Desert Gardens

Desert Gardens

Photographs by
Melba Levick

Text by
Gary Lyons

RIZZOLI
NEW YORK

First published in the United States of America by
Rizzoli International Publications, Inc.
300 Park Avenue South
New York, NY 10010

ISBN: 0-8478-2187-0
LC: 99-85859

Cover: Huntington Desert Garden

Designed by Judy Geib

Printed and bound in Singapore

Pages 2-3: A medley of flowering Schick echinopsis hybrids growing at the Huntington.

Contents

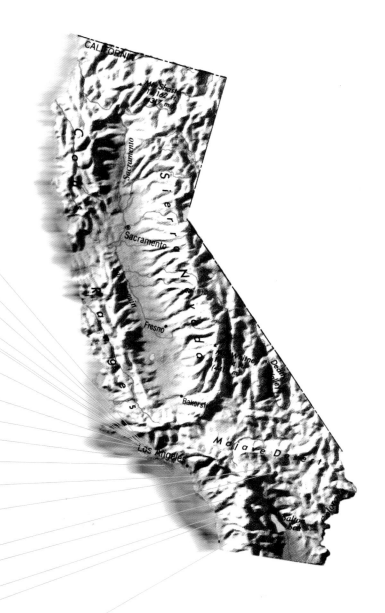

Introduction: The Desert Garden in Southern California, 8

Gunter Schwartz Garden, Santa Barbara, 18

Frank Jordano Garden, Santa Barbara, 28

Ganna Walska Lotusland, Montecito, 36

Gary Lyons Garden, Burbank, 50

Fick Garden, Pasadena, 58

Los Angeles City Zoo, Griffith Park, Los Angeles, 64

Rancho Santa Ana Botanic Garden, Claremont, 70

Huntington Desert Garden, San Marino, 76

San Gabriel Mission, San Gabriel, 94

Getty Center Cactus Garden, Los Angeles, 100

Modelo Shales, Pacific Palisades, 106

Serra Gardens, Malibu, 114

Moorten Botanical Gardens, Palm Springs, 122

Living Desert Wildlife and Animal Park, Palm Desert, 132

O'Neill Garden, San Juan Capistrano, 140

Patrick Anderson Garden, Fallbrook, 150

Phil Favel Garden, Escondido, 158

Balboa Park Cactus Gardens, San Diego, 166

Index, 174

Directory and Bibliography, 176

The Desert Garden in Southern California
by Gary Lyons

The eighteen Southern California desert gardens in this book represent a design genre that demonstrates how their owners and caretakers, often with little more than good intuition and a sense of color and proportion, can create beautiful gardens. This is especially the case in the private gardens: few of them are designed according to landscape architecture standards; instead, they represent extensions of the greatly enriched lives of their owners and cultivators. However, the desert or cactus garden does have its dark side—the threat of serious pain posed by some brutally spiny cacti. Hieronymus Bosch may have used some of the specimens in this book to depict Hell, while Fragonard may have selected others, spiny or spineless, to serve as luxuriant flora along the road to Paradise.

Some of the gardens look like attempts to transcend art and landscape, or simply to ignore it. Except for the Getty Center, most have not been designed as displays for instant effect. Several, like the Favel garden of aloes, are collections, or include collections, of unusual species—rare in cultivation and perhaps endangered in the wild. This gives the gardener of succulent landscapes the added purpose of attempting to slow the ever-accelerating process of extinction: a biologically retrograde condition that threatens more than humanity; as it gnaws at the very existence of evolution and its corollary, speciation. Many gardens, whether attractive or unattractive, suggest the designer's, gardener's, or collector's awareness that he or she is participating in an *ex situ* conservation experiment: if the plants become extinct in the wild, at least the caretaker has made an effort to conserve them. The effort works so long as the plants are well tended and handed on to others. This theme is often stated or implied in the ark-like makeup and mission of many of the gardens.

Keeping such gardens growing from one generation to the next, particularly those that include documented specialty collections, is a challenge. These gardens have an inherent complexity that makes it difficult to keep plants alive, preserve any associated data, and see that they are distributed to those best able to conserve and hand them over to the next generation. The Huntington Desert Garden, approaching its hundredth year, is the oldest garden in the book, but few of its original collections exist, and maintaining survival strategies through time is its greatest challenge.

I have spent most of my life growing and studying cacti and other succulents and have become a champion of their conservation, if for no other reason than being aware that their advocates are few. The gardens in this book were created by owners and caretakers whose intense enthusiasm and determination not only resulted in exotic expressions of beauty but also, perhaps unknowingly, in botanical arks that nurture rare and endangered species that may never again be found in the wild. Two gardens, the Huntington and the Los Angeles Zoo, are officially designated rescue centers for confiscated and salvaged succulents protected by the U.S. Endangered Species Act and the Convention on International Trade in Endangered Species (CITES). All others have no official conservation role, except that their owners collect, grow, and love their plants. Some do keep records, an activity combined with horticultural practices that could establish a new garden ethic, conservation gardening. This approach, coupled with botanic garden collections management techniques, is getting an added push by increased enforcement of national and international plant collecting and export laws, making it difficult, and in some cases impossible, to introduce species from the wild. The Convention on Biological Diversity has made it easier for some countries to refuse to let plants or seeds leave their country for whatever reason. In developing nations, where habitat destruction is rapidly accelerating, this may imperil species even further.

I worry about the future of these eighteen gardens. Private gardens rarely outlive their owners. Just by glancing through old issues of garden magazines it becomes clear that collections and landscapes are ephemeral. What happens to the very rare, unusual, and documented plants? Heirs, executors, and real-estate agents do not take kindly to cactus collections and gardens; they are usually booted off the property. Permanent collections like those in the Huntington Desert Garden often benefit from the dispersal of these gardens and collections, but there are no guarantees. Not all the gardens fit the botanical ark concept. Certainly it was not a motivation for building the Getty garden. Here the motive was to give voice to the dramatic color and geometric beauty of the desert; in its wake the botanical ark entered. The plants became their own conservation advocates.

Personal expression and conservation are not the only points of view. This book attempts to illustrate the development of design concepts, some standard in desert gardening and landscaping, some artistic, some absolutely nuts. A few of the traditional styles have become interchangeable clichés; for example, the drought-tolerant garden, xeriscape garden, desert garden, cactus garden, subtropical desert garden, Mediterranean garden, and mission garden. All of these styles, however defined, contribute elements to what I term the Southern California desert garden genre. This stylistic classification might be unacceptable to designers who prefer to steer away from cacti, but if artists can paint in a California style—the plein air—then cactus gardeners can certainly plant in a California landscape style.

In this new millennium, Southern California will come to terms with the issue that has dogged it from the beginning: availability of water. The area is renowned for its historic image as an archetypal example of terrestrial paradise. Much of that image was carefully crafted by real-estate salespeople, the railroads, and any number of well-meaning or greedy boosters and hucksters. Benjamin Truman's *Semi-Tropical California*, Theodore S. Van Dyke's *Southern California*, and Charles Nordhoff's *California: A Book for Travellers and Settlers* are samples of railroad- and real-estate-subsidized accounts of growing gardens, citrus, food crops, and so on. True chronicles of winter frosts, summer heat waves, and drought were suppressed. The idea was to buy land, plant grapes, citrus, and wheat, and watch your bank account grow. If that would not work because of poor health, then you were encouraged to settle in one of Southern California's new health-resort communities. There were books, such as F.C.S. Sanders' *California as a Health Resort* and P.C. Remondino's *The Mediterranean Shores of America*, where temperature and other climatic records were massaged to a degree of mildness that is scarcely credible. The salubrious climate, gentle air, health-giving waters, and many lovely gardens were just the tonic for nearly all chronic ailments.

Toward the end of the nineteenth century the terrestrial-paradise idea gained momentum from a new selling angle: massive irrigation projects. William E. Smythe, in his book *The Arid Conquest of America*, urged the American empire to conquer the desert and make it bloom by way of federally subsidized dams and irrigation canals. To Smythe and his world, the desert (his desert included any undeveloped area in Southern California) was to be transformed into usable land as a matter of great national urgency. To make his case Smythe used a photo of White Park in Riverside pointing out that the water canal in the foreground brings the water to create greenery, thereby rescuing the desert from oblivion. However, in the fuzzy background of the photo one can make out a cactus garden, then the pride of Riverside, which touted it as the largest public cactus garden in the world. The boosters, lobbyists, and land developers apparently saw cacti and deserts as threats. Whereas the public, my grandparents included, were fascinated by cacti and other desert plants that were significant elements in the designed landscape.

Developers and their supporters gave little thought to what might be gained from water conservation. Their only concern was to get water to the drylands; any part of Southern California without their preferred eastern garden plants, e.g., magnolia, lilac, daylily, and canna, was seen as desert, and new settlers from the East Coast and Midwest were happy to oblige. Only the Anglo-Saxon culture and their plants could redeem the desert and make it a real Garden of Eden. That image worked. It brought the farmers, the retirees, and the ill, and for a time the terrestrial paradise became more paradisiacal than in the days of the missions and haciendas. Southern California's oak woodlands and chaparral were transformed into some of the finest, most picturesque farmland, parkland, and rangeland in the world. The transformation was brief, however.

From the botany and biodiversity standpoint, the railroads and the land speculators were right: more species and varieties of plants can be grown in Southern California than anywhere in the world. The problem is that the speculators were looking far beyond agriculture and large gardens. In 1913, the California Aqueduct brought water to the Los Angeles area, especially the San Fernando Valley, not for agriculture but for planned residential subdivisions—today known for gridlock and smog. Yet, in spite of Southern California's mushrooming population, polluted air, and traffic congestion, fleeting glimpses of the terrestrial paradise remain and will be seen in this book.

There is certainly a need for a renewed awareness and appreciation of the sculpturesque charms found in a cactaceous landscape. Many of the gardens in this book are living proof that landscaping with so-called water-wise succulents does not contradict the longing for prelapsarian topography. One can and does feel a sense of awe—of being in a special place—in these Southern Californian gardens. There is something numinous about the light and the way it intensifies the strange yet boldly geometric forms. If some people find the plants—because of their spines or shape—less than alluring, they will surely be hooked and become budding cactophiles by their incomparable flowers. Certainly the O'Neill garden, complemented by the nearly pristine Southern California coast chaparral and oak woodland, expresses the sense of a found paradise. Hopefully some of the gardens I have selected also demonstrate this numinous quality.

Cactus gardens are not for everyone. Who hears of anyone putting in a cactus garden so they can have a place to relax? I relax in my cactus garden by working in it, making certain I take time to admire the endless procession of flowers and new growth. Perhaps the perception of the uninitiated that cacti suggest discomfort and pain—H.E. Huntington's association—is why today's landscape architects make little use of cacti and why it is often difficult to locate in the trade mature specimens suitable for landscaping.

Except for the Living Desert Wildlife and Animal Park and the Moorten Botanic Garden, both in the driest part of the Sonoran Desert, this book celebrates the Southern California desert garden genre. This eccentric, certainly eclectic, form of the subtropical garden in the context of a Mediterranean climate borrows the plants but leaves the desert behind. Actually, I seldom recommend planting local desert plants such as Mojave Desert chollas, barrel cacti, hedgehogs, and Joshua trees in the coastal regions. Mercifully for children and emergency room physicians, the Mojave succulent flora is adapted to extreme desert conditions and performs best within those hellacious borders. The succulent plant palette found in the southland's many desert gardens samples the plant-life of the deserts and drylands of the world. Most of the columnar cacti and terrestrial bromeliads we see are from

Mexico, Brazil, Argentina, and Peru—from the high Andes to rocky outcroppings in tropical grasslands. The globular cacti are from our Southwest deserts: the Mojave, Sonoran, and Chihuahuan. Most agaves, yuccas, and many forms of cacti and soft crassulaceous succulents come from thorn scrub and drylands in subtropical and tropical Mexico. Aloes and euphorbias emanate from dry savannas and deserts throughout Africa and the Arabian subcontinent.

Years ago at the Huntington, I began to wonder why a desert garden included only cacti and succulents. Every spring a few naturalized California poppies emerged among the agaves and yuccas in the lower desert garden, and I wondered why there should not be more wildflowers and desert trees and shrubs. Not only do herbaceous and leafy plants provide extra color, but they also dance and enliven the garden as the late afternoon sea breezes sweep over the San Gabriel Valley, whereas the fortress-like agaves and cacti do not move a bit; they are totally unresponsive to wind. The wildflower notion did not wash with my superiors. However, we did plant out numerous cassia shrubs, desert and savanna trees that add warmth and softness to the landscape. These also serve the utilitarian purpose of providing afternoon cover for the shade-loving succulents. In the Mojave Desert the herbaceous plant strategy works very well in desert gardens because few soft succulents, such as aloe, crassula, and echeveria, will tolerate the blistering heat and cold winter winds.

The private gardens presented in this book are the pride and joy of their owners, who are avid succulent plant enthusiasts and are fortunate to have the space to make their botanical and horticultural dreams a reality. Most of the gardens are unplanned plantscapes. Patrick Anderson calls his magnificent display "a garden of happy accidents." Even the O'Neill garden betrays a love of puttering, and no plant goes unnoticed or unappreciated. Only in the Getty are there significant walls, stairs, and pavement that affect the feeling of the cactus plantings. What most of these gardens have in common is the great electrifying diversity of color, form,

and species—common and rare—and a sense of their owner's joy and pride, which sings out to the visitor.

The Huntington is the sine qua non of public desert gardens, and many regard it as the largest and finest in the world. It began small, but by the time William Hertrich, its founder, retired in 1949 it was internationally known as both the ultimate in cactus landscaping and desert botanical gardens. The desert garden genre is a recent development and a landscape style that does not trace its roots to English landscape gardening, but the English certainly had something to do with it. Collecting cacti goes back to the late Renaissance. Linnaeus, in the eighteenth century, described cactus species mainly based on plants he had seen in European collections. The nineteenth century saw a flourish of collecting and collection building in Europe. Colonial expansion brought newly discovered species to eager collectors and their improved greenhouses. In the United States, collecting cacti did not emerge as an established hobby until the later years of the nineteenth century following on the heels of railroad surveys and the settling of the West. There were collectors and their trophies, but garden making with succulents was nonexistent to very rare. The settling of the Southwest, particularly Southern California, saw a push to improve irrigation, not just for farming, but also for growing the plants traditional to eastern and English gardens. The lush look came with the Europeans. They just needed to add water.

It is a mystery where cactus and succulent gardens first appeared. If it occurred in the desert Southwest, like Phoenix or Tucson, they may have gone unrecorded. Even today there are homes in the Tucson area where it takes a good eye to distinguish the planted cacti from the Sonoran Desert context. It could be that the first real desert gardens that were planted with some overall concept in mind were within the natural range of the native species.

Gardening with cacti and succulents evolved, in part, with the emergence of landscape gardening in Southern California; however, by the 1880s there was a lively trade in wild plants collected in Mexico and throughout the western United States that serviced what had become an American "cactus craze." A plant catalogue (ca. 1897) of Anna B. Nickel's Arcadia cactus nursery in Laredo, Texas, reveals an inventory of Chihuahuan and Sonoran Desert cacti that would dwarf that of a modern catalogue. Unlike today, specialty cactus nurseries at that time did not grow cacti from seed; all plants were dug in their natural habitat. In Southwest nurseries, few exotic succulents were offered for sale; nearly all cacti were mature collected plants, few from Africa until the 1890s and only a handful from South America. The deserts were being plundered, but most of the plants were shipped to collectors, not landscapers, on the East Coast and in Europe. In the Southwest, residences often used specimens of *Agave americana* and mission cactus as accents. These two succulents also served utilitarian purposes. The Indian fig, or mission cactus, was a food source, boundary marker, and natural fence to repel intruders. More readily obtainable native cacti and succulents, such as the coast cholla, as well as yuccas, like the Lord's candle, were also incorporated into the home landscape simply because they were easy to find, grew everywhere, and needed no water.

Unlike the mission gardens and those of the accompanying Hispanic period, the gardens influenced by the East Coast settlers and English landscape garden styles were for aesthetic display. However, the realities of Mediterranean climatic factors, such as unpredictable rainfall and often semidesert heat encouraged limited appreciation of xerophytes, or plants structurally adapted for life with a limited water supply, including succulents, though most homeowners and their gardeners opted for more water for nonsucculent exotics. A few succulents were associated with the California missions. Others were brought by white settlers before and during the gold rush era. The century plant (*Agave americana*), medicinal aloe (*Aloe vera*), and the mission or Indian fig cactus (*Opuntia ficus indica* and *O. megacantha*) were utilized on mission grounds; *Aloe arborescens*, native to South Africa, was brought to California by American or British travellers. Farmers and ranchers recognized that if plants carried their own water supply in their leaves and stems they would survive blistering summer heat and require little or none of the precious irrigation water. Water for lush landscapes was in limited supply in the Los Angeles area until 1915, when the Owens River Aqueduct was completed.

There is another dimension to the development of interest in cacti and succulents: beginning in the early eighteenth century, plant explorers who trekked the drylands of southern Africa sent back to Europe many interesting novelty succulents and created a high demand for exotic 'stove' plants. Nurseries in England, Germany, and most other western European countries fattened their catalogues with new aloes, euphorbias, haworthias, mesembs, and stapeliads for greenhouse collections. By 1840, a cactus craze—a veritable tulipomania with spines—hit England. Across the Atlantic, the botanical discoveries of Dr. George Englemann and others from the military reconaissances and railroad surveys in the American Southwest, created an instant demand from the East Coast and Europe for the native cacti, which overnight became botanical gold. Not everyone agreed with Major John C. Fremont, who during a march through the Mojave Desert in 1844 remarked that the Joshua tree is "the most repulsive tree in the plant kingdom." Collectors then, and now for that matter, paid any price for newly discovered species. A living rock cactus, *Ariocarpus kotschubeyanus*, newly discovered in Mexico, brought a price in Europe equal to that of its weight in gold. From a conservationist point of view, it was best that the California Argonauts who stampeded west in search of gold knew nothing of the green gold growing along their route.

By the 1850s a nursery trade was flourishing in California. In 1853, Warren and Sons in Sacramento advertised cacti in their catalogues, and several other nursery and seed companies, such as William C. Walker of San Francisco and Stephen Nolan of Oakland, followed suit in introducing plants from Mexico and Africa. In Southern California's terrestrial paradise, agaves became popular in gardens and were often referred to as "hot-weather plants."

Cactus displays, plantings, and fully developed gardens began to appear in Southern California in the 1880s. Ranches and homes in the San Gabriel Valley and Los Angeles had cactus beds, often planted with native chollas, barrel cacti, ocotillo, and agaves. One exceptional display that survives in contemporary photos was the cactus garden at Albert S. White Park in Riverside. This two-acre cactus garden, part of the city's municipal park and within walking distance of the famous Riverside Mission Inn, was laid out and planted in 1893 by Swiss garden designer F.P. Hosp, who had worked for Adolph Haage in Erfurt, probably the largest cactus nursery in the world in the nineteenth century. Hosp acquired over three-hundred species of specimen cacti and succulents, mostly from Europe (probably through Haage), and his garden was ranked by the Smithsonian Institution as among the very best cactus collections in the country. In fact, it was ranked with Missouri Botanical Garden and the New York Botanical Garden in importance. The White Park garden may have displayed the initial introductions of many of the South American night-blooming cerei. The garden was an intensive display crowded with columnar South American cacti that must have kept caretakers at bay—a mix of stiff geometric plant design bordering rock—lined dirt paths, with horticulturally irresponsible juxtapositions of specimen cacti collected in the Mojave and Sonoran Deserts. Before long, Hosp's cactus creation succumbed to a fate shared by many unfenced municipal gardens: theft and vandalism.

When the garden was dismantled in the early 1900s, a number of the large specimens were brought by wagon to the new Huntington Desert Garden. In fact, the early plantings at the Huntington testify to the fact that by 1907 many native and nonnative cacti and succulents were grown in gardens. Huntington commissioned Hertrich to scour Southern California gardens and nurseries for the finest specimens to plant in the desert garden. Hertrich must have also depleted many of Huntington's properties (he had numerous holdings throughout Southern California) of their specimen succulents. In fact, the Huntington and many other estate gardens from that era benefited from their own field collecting in the local desert and Mexico.

The 1890s saw establishment of a number of nurseries specializing in exotic and native cacti for the collector and the local homeowner. In Hollywood, Lyon and Cobbe grew thousands of cacti on ten acres of open fields, much like large wholesale growers do today in San Diego County. Lyon and Cobbe, Stengel, and Weinberg supplied the Huntington in the early 1900s. These and many other Southern California nurseries also exported new and rare species to Europe. Specialty nurseries, such and Johnson's Water and Cactus Gardens, begun in the 1930s, focused less on plants collected in the Southwest and more on growing imported seed and vegetative propagations of succulents for the collector

and the greenhouse. The introduction of South African succulents, such as aloes, euphorbias, and mesembs, dramatically altered the look of many Southern California succulents gardens and greatly expanded the diversity of species and their forms.

In 1929, the beginning of the Great Depression not only put a restraint on the great cactus gardens (and on all extravagant gardens, for that matter), but also saw the beginning of two magazines for the cactus and succulent enthusiast. One was the *Journal of the Cactus and Succulent Society of America*, published by the Abbey San Encino Press in Los Angeles. The other was *Desert Plant Life*, edited by Ellen Rooksby and published out of Pasadena.

Scott Haselton, *Cactus and Succulent*'s editor, assisted by William Hertrich and numerous influential hobbyists and botanists, founded the Cactus and Succulent Society of America. It was the CSSA that performed a great service in popularizing cacti and succulents for the collector and for the Southwest gardener. Haselton published numerous titles on cacti and succulents, including several definitive monographs, but he is perhaps best known for his long-in-print books *Cacti for the Amateur* and *Succulents for the Amateur*. Both the society and its journal weathered the Depression and wars, and are still with us today. Though the original readership of the journal may have been concentrated in California, there were a few articles on landscaping with succulents in other regions. It was Haselton's desire to create a magazine that would address the needs of the hobbyist collector by relating more to plant identification and collection maintenance.

Desert Plant Life, founded the same year as the CSSA journal, was not supported by a society and was primarily the creation of its founder and editor, Ellen Rooksby. Its editorial policy was not connected to any hobby organization and did not maintain a narrow editorial focus on select groups of plants. Surprisingly, it is in *Desert Plant Life*, a magazine that did not survive, that we see a linkage between the love of the desert and the love of landscape gardening. Because collecting rare and unusual plants was not the primary focus of the magazine, there were numerous articles on gardens as well as on nonsucculent plants. *Desert Plant Life* had an influence on gardening with succulents in Southern California and in a sense complimented the CSSA's exclusive focus on individual species of succulents, descriptions of new species, taxonomic revision and research, and collecting specimens in the wild. The magazine also played a strong advocacy role in exposing collector and other abuses, such as the Los Angeles cactus candy industry, which led to depletion of the native barrel cacti in local deserts.

The inaugural issue of *Desert Plant Life* began with a plea for desert conservation and, under Rooksby, called for the creation of desert reserves and a halt to the plundering of cacti from the nearby deserts. This matter was not taken seriously by the CSSA until the 1970s and when collecting in the wild came under the scrutiny of the U.S. Endangered Species Act and the Convention on International Trade in Endangered Species, better known by the acronym CITES. Implementation impacted the collection of rare and endangered succulents by making it illegal to import protected plants and seeds without the necessary permits. The United States has aggressively enforced plant laws in order to protect habitat. Recently, with or without U.S. cooperation, the Convention on Biological Diversity (CBD) has empowered developing nations to enforce their own collecting and plant export laws. These measures have brought about a heightened awareness of habitat depletion and have caused the nursery trade to put a far greater emphasis on seed and vegetative propagation.

The hobbyist-collector is not alone in being affected by the permit process. In the southwestern desert there exists a lively trade in specimen-size native cacti for landscaping. Large compass barrels, hedgehog clumps, teddy-bear chollas, Joshua trees, Spanish daggar yuccas, and ocotillo, are a common sight in most urban areas from El Paso to Las Vegas, Phoenix, Tucson, Palm Springs, and Los Angeles. The first response is to conclude that someone is pirating plants off the desert; however, this is not necessarily the case. If legally removed, a plant will have a large permit tag and seal tied to it. In Arizona, many prime cactus habitats are on the drawing board for urban development, mining operations, and road and freeway construction. This means the plants are either bulldozed or sold to nurseries and landscapers. In large areas, such as Arizona's Navajo Dam, the usable plants are auctioned to the highest bidder.

For some species, such as the cottontop cactus (*Echinocactus polycephalus*), it may make little difference which option is chosen—in either case the plant dies. However, many field-collected or -harvested cacti and succulents will survive in a garden if they are treated as plants in shock and given care to see that their damaged roots are trimmed and that they are sparingly watered. It may take one to two years to establish a compass barrel or hedgehog cactus, and up to four years for a saguaro. Winter or spring rains help things along. Cacti transplanted from a humid desert to a dry desert, say from central Arizona to Las Vegas, will require summer sun protection and some water. Care must be given saguaros and barrel cacti to see that they are properly "compassed", i.e., planted with the same side of the plant receiving maximum exposure as it did in the wild.

Not all plant introduction was in the hands of local collectors and nursery owners. The U.S. Department of Agriculture (USDA) was for years a primary supplier of new and exotic succulent plants to private gardens. Frustrated in its effort in the 1890s to build an acclimatization garden in what is now Los Angeles' Griffith Park, the USDA resorted to providing large ranches and estate gardens seed and plants. Government botanists explored remote areas of many parts of the world in search of economic, medicinal, and ornamental plant species. Cacti and succulents considered worthy of testing in Southern California were sent to the Huntington Ranch, the Arthur Letts estate (Letts had assembled what was perhaps the largest cactus collection in the United States by the 1920s), and other gardens. William Hertrich kept careful records, sending reports to Washington describing the performance and passing judgment on the garden-worthiness of the USDA introductions. Many survive to this day.

Foreign botanic gardens made a significant contribution to the Southern California succulent plant palette. For example, many of the aloes and agaves in the Huntington were obtained by Hertrich from La Mortola, a garden on the Italian Riviera. La Mortola was begun by English industrialist Sir Thomas Hanbury in 1867, several years before succulent gardens became fashionable in Southern California. La Mortola provided many plants still in the garden today that had proven their garden-worthiness in a

Mediterranean climate. At the time the Hertrich was developing the Huntington Desert Garden, Alwin Berger, La Mortola's chief botanist, was the eminent authority on succulents. Not only did Berger provide many valuable introductions to the Huntington and probably other Southern California estate gardens, but he also provided the Huntington with a master landscape gardener: his son, Fritz Berger.

At over ninety years, the Huntington has the oldest extant desert or cactus garden in Southern California. Within its prickly borders remain evidences of innovative planting concepts—a living textbook of design that teaches as it grows. The Huntington set the pace for the design concepts that appear in many gardens today. While some gardens, like the San Gabriel Mission's cactus garden, are cacophonous assemblages of succulents sharing a common space, most gardens demonstrate an awareness of the aesthetic and practical value of raised beds and rock or rockery layout. The association of succulents with intensive use of stone sets a naturalistic tone to the garden; it makes the cactus garden more like a garden than the more primitive flat gravel beds that show off specimens. In 1929, two years after Huntington's death and on the eve of the library, art gallery, and botanic garden's opening debut, William Hertrich created what today is one of the largest cactus rockeries in the world. He was among the first to apply the English rock garden concept to cactus and succulent garden design and certainly the first to apply it on such a massive scale. Rock gardens were first popularized in Europe by the Frenchman Jean Attiret, who wrote about the rock gardens he had seen during his travels in China in the early eighteenth century. The rock garden concept was adopted by English and Scottish gardeners, but it was reserved for alpines and small tufted herbaceous perennials.

A NOTE ON TERMINOLOGY

Some clarification of terms is needed to help understand the garden descriptions in this book. Because of the complex morphologies of succulents, I have attempted to simplify terms and concepts as much as possible, but some incursion into the language of botany—or botanese—is unavoidable. For starters, cactus refers to a natural family (the *Cactaceae*) of mostly succulent plants. Cacti (cactus and cactuses are also used to signify the plural form) are stem succulents, rarely leafy, characterized by highly specialized structures visible on the plant surface called areoles. The areole is a highly modified leaf bud that is protected by wool and from which emerge spines, bristles, hairs, flower, fruit, and offsets. Cactus flowers are solitary, quite showy, and usually produce a berry-like many-seeded fleshy fruit. Twenty-five-hundred species of cacti and two hundred genera occur in the Western Hemisphere, but a few tropical epiphytic species are found in tropical Africa and Madagascar. For the sake of brevity, cactus garden is used here to describe a garden of cacti and other succulents. For convenience, succulents may be used to indicate cacti and other succulents; after all, a cactus is one of the other succulents. Succulent refers to an adaptive strategy, found in over thirty plant families, and is not a family or genus of related plants. Therefore succulent is the all-inclusive term.

I apologize for the excessive use of botanical names. It reveals the fact that many of the plants are so uncommon that common epithets do not exist. If they were required, I would have to make up the names, names that would be known to no one but me. Committed plant fanatics like myself rarely use common names; an outsider listening to conversations between collectors and amateur botanists would probably hear incomprehensible word salads. Perhaps someday the plants illustrated and discussed in this book will be so popular that there will be common names for them. In closing it should be noted that during Southern California's Golden Age of Horticulture (the 1880's), the garden, botany, and plant identification books were rather technical—emphasizing botanical names—and, puzzlingly, most of them were written for children and teenagers. Have we come a long way?

Gunther Schwartz Garden, Santa Barbara

The incredible diversity of exotic, tropical, and rarely seen plants in Gunther Schwartz's rambling paradise garden in the hills above Santa Barbara defies description. The Schwartz succulent garden is part of a veritable ark of botanical diversity. Gunther's love of unusual plants developed when he lived in Hawaii, but when he relocated to Santa Barbara, he spent the next eighteeen years setting out plant after plant and, perhaps inadvertently, developed the modern equivalent of Dr. Franceschi's famous Garden of Acclimatization in the Santa Barbara foothills over a century ago. To tour this garden is to tour the plant kingdom—it is a botanical garden for one. Linnaeus would have loved it.

The idea of a cactus garden grew out of the need for a buffer between a three-hundred-acre nature reserve and Schwartz's three-acre parcel. He needed a barrier both to retard fire and to prevent hikers from trekking through his property. Gunther installed a two-to-three-foot retaining wall on the east edge, the uphill side, for the full length of the four-hundred-foot-long driveway. The material is a medium traditional in earlier Southern California hardscapes: stacked chunks of broken cement sidewalk. The pebbly texture often works very well, especially if used in conjunction with granite river rock. Gunther says these are not just ordinary chunks of sidewalk. "This sidewalk came from the old Santa Barbara Biltmore Hotel and a lot of famous people walked on it," he says. The hillside continues to slope upward from the retaining wall, and on it he has built a rockery, as long as the wall, of native sandstone boulders. This impressive rockery displays only a portion of the amazing succulent garden.

Once the garden was planted, Gunther discovered it catered a gourmet diet to armies of gophers camped in the wilderness park. When he found that gophers also relished the soft-pointed Spanish dagger yucca (*Yucca gloriosa*), he planted them along the edge of his property. Now the gophers have no incentive to chew any further into the garden.

Gunther Schwartz's subtropical paradise consists of several theme gardens and displays in addition to cacti and

Previous page: O'Neill Ranch desert garden with part of the ranch in the background.

In the foreground, flowering lampranthus; top: flowering clumps of *Aloe nobilis*; center top: *Opuntia spinulifera*.

succulents: orchids; palms and cycads; Mediterranean plants; aloes; a kalanchoe display; a bromeliad garden; and dozens of tropical trees and shrubs never recommended for Southern California landscaping. These gardens testify to the fact that gardeners, not garden handbooks, are the last word in what grows best where. Here it is possible to admire an enormous fan-shaped Traveler's palm (*Ravenala madagascariensis*) or be scared out one's shoes and socks by a too-close encounter with the squirting cucumber (*Ecballium elaterium*), a Mediterranean native that contains a chemical highly effective as a male contraceptive. Gunther also has an ombu tree (*Phytolacca dioica x P. weberbaueri*), but not the one native to the Argentine pampas; rather it is a hybrid super tree that probably originated from seed of the Argentine ombu at the Huntington. It is so enormous—its swollen base eventually would fill a small yard—that it may have to be removed.

It is important to know flowering seasons for cacti and succulents. In June most aloes and small cacti are finished, but the flashy genus *Lampranthus* hangs on. Gunther makes liberal use of pink and crimson mesembs, which he pulls up yearly. He does not bother to replant; they simply reseed themselves. In June, ground-cover *lampranthus* and stone tie together the huge rockery; of course, there is the yucca backdrop assisted by sculpted clumps of foxtail agave (*Agave attenuata*). An old aeonium hybrid (there are many and most are unnamed) grows in clumping rosettes. Inland, they stay green leaved; here the tips of the spoon-shaped leaves are cheerfully reddish. Flowering for most of the spring is a coral aloe hybrid, very common in Southern California, but for some reason, nobody ever named it.

The Schwartz garden is packed with rare specimens of South American cacti and caudiciforms from Africa, including a magnificent specimen of the so-called Madagascar palm (*Pachypodium lameri*). Though common, it is growing into a very unusual bottle shape. Echeverias and other soft succulents are found throughout, even featured in a well-rusted and decaying wheelbarrow.

In spite of this being a private garden, Gunther takes an active interest in providing a place where people can see and learn about plants. Horticulture societies, garden clubs, and senior groups are regularly invited to see the garden, and Gunther gets great satisfaction when he inspires people to dare to garden with their own hands.

Spring flowering *trichocereus* (*echinopsis*) hybrid.

Aloe display along driveway and gopher food (*Yucca gloriosa*) in the background.

Aeoniums, aloes, and agaves;
right foreground: pink flowering *lampranthus*.

Peruvian Borzicactus
(Hildewintera) aureispinus.

Foreground: *aeonium* hybrid;
left and top: Foxtail Agave (*Agave attentuata*).
Aloe striata in the background.

The Coral Aloe (*Aloe striata*) at peak flowering.

Exquisite specimen of *Pachypodium lameri*,
one of the so-called Madagascar palms.

The spreading coast, live oaks, and enormous chunks of sandstone persuaded Frank Jordano to purchase the hillside Santa Barbara property. It was his landscape gardener's eye that recognized the scattered sandstone boulders as a natural rockery for cacti. Some of the sandstone boulders were enormous and had been tumbling out of the Santa Ynez Mountains, Santa Barbara's rocky backdrop, through the millennia. Most Santa Barbara gardens feature this brownish rock: design with it or dynamite it! This stone is such a dominant a visual effect that landscapes of imported stone look odd and out of place.

The Jordano garden covers an acre, most of it facing the street, from which it can be comfortably viewed. The house sits among oaks at the top of the property. The garden's perimeter is planted with large, flowering clumps of echinopsis similar to the Huntington's Schick hybrids. Passersby often stop to admire the showy flowers, Frank says twice a year a couple from Carmel, two hundred miles up the coast, drive down just to see the brilliant flowers in his garden. Like Phil Favel's aloe garden (pages 158–165), paths are mirages and a walk in the desert garden can be quite painful, yet the cactus collector's enthusiasm for plants rarely extends to pathwork. The focus here is on making room for the plants, getting to them is something to worry about later.

The Jordano garden is a great example of a cactus enthusiast's garden, a landscape that continuously evolves as Frank's interests in one group of plants moves on to another. A 1929 *Desert Plant Life* writer gave this advice to any cactus enthusiast who tries a hand at landscaping: "If you cannot picture [the] effect you would like, go to the desert and find just the spot you would enjoy having at home, then sketch or photograph it...The nook you will most admire will doubtless be some rought [sic] bit of ground, well strewn with rock, age-old and weather-worn, and standing out like sentinels against the hand of time are many stickery, treacherous, yet altogether lovely cacti." Not a bad idea, but Jordano's garden, like most cactus and succulent gardens today, is not the exclusive domain of cacti: its look is dramatically altered by

Foreground: clumps of flowering Pride of Madeira (*Echium fastuosum*); left: *borzicactus*; center: flowering *Aloe africana* and African Iris (*Dietes vegeta*).

the inclusion of New Zealand flax (*Phormium tenax*) and Australian kangaroo paw, both forming dense masses of sword-leaved foliage and impressive branched inflorescences. Surprisingly, their effect harmonizes effectively with the statuesque columnar cacti and is an instance where experimental gardening paid off.

From the porch the hazy late-afternoon sun ignites the spiny cacti below into a warm golden glow, reminiscent not of some horrific Dantesque scene but of an image of a lost era—a California pastoral setting. At Frank Jordano's garden, one gets a sense of being at the historic center of Southern California horticulture. Just a couple of miles away are the Santa Barbara Mission; the Santa Barbara Botanic Garden; the Santa Barbara Acclimatization Association (now Franceschi Park); in earlier times, the botanic garden nurseries of Joseph Sexton; not to mention the nursery of Elwood Cooper, who introduced eucalyptus to Southern California. There are many examples and traditions to suggest that Southern California horticulture has its roots in Santa Barbara and lives on in Frank Jordano's and Gunther Schwartz's (pages 18–27) love of exotic gardening and gardens. In a mild climate like Santa Barbara, where it seems anything can grow, novel plant combinations are common. There are no hard-and-fast rules governing what one plants in a Santa Barbara garden. Cactus and succulent landscapes are a more substantial component of the garden tradition here than in Los Angeles.

The oak trees that both shade and frame the house serve as cover for numerous specimen bromeliads, epiphytic cacti, and rarely seen baby blue *pilosocereus* from Brazil. Pilosocerei are glaucous blue-stemmed columnar cacti distantly related to the old man cactus from Mexico and present a most unusual and unexpected association with a grayish wall. The bluish color is in part enhanced by a waxy cuticle that covers the epidermis to prevent excessive water loss. If these cacti do not get your attention, the bats that pollinate them will.

The bouldered garden features many colorful and unusual aloe hybrids. Those suitable for the landscape garden seldom make their way beyond the walls of botanic gardens, where many of them originate. Botanic gardens may feature medium to large hybrid aloes such as *Aloe* 'Sailor's Warning' or *A.* 'William Hertrich', but sadly these have not been distributed to the general public. This is not due to reluctance by the Huntington or anyone else but

Left foreground, *Cleistocactus wendeliorum*;
above: *Opuntia robusta*; center: *Aloe mutabilis*.

Hybrid echinopsis in flower. Left: *Agave ferox*, a
pulque agave.

Overleaf: Detail of the hybrid echinopsis

is the result of few collectors and gardeners knowing of their existence. Frank Jordano has the space for them and there are no complaints about his beautiful orange-flowered aloe hybrid, possibly a cross between the coral-flowered A. *thraskii* and the huge tree aloe, A. *bainesii*. Unfortunately, Jordano's specimen defies proper identification, and its hybridizer is unknown; though it could have originated in Santa Barbara. Years ago David Verity, manager of the Mildred Mathias Botanical Garden, made a number of interesting aloe crosses, some of which still thrive at the Huntington. These are large plants, not for the small garden, but rather for a large spacious and sunny garden, like Frank's.

Keeping track of the names of hybrids, and all other plants for that matter, is a very important conservation issue but is a touchy subject with many gardeners. A landscaped garden with plants properly named is a rarity. Labels usually detract from the owner's appreciation of the plants and are a problem for maintenance. At the Huntington, shrubby aloes, groundcover mesembs, and sprawling puyas and agaves stealthily swallow identification tags, and the identity of some specimens may remain

a mystery until they die or are dug up. Those who possess large gardens with many mature specimens of exotic succulents should make some kind of effort to maintain records for conservation purposes and to assure that hybrid species and their correct names are not lost. Scores of once-popular hybrid succulents have become lost simply because their labels are missing, placed on some other plant, or because a caretaker failed to remember the correct name. Frank Jordano has many full-grown specimens of South American columnar cacti not often seen outside botanic collections. In Europe, they would most likely be kept in undersized pots and crammed into a small greenhouse.

The Jordano garden reveals an interest in the night-blooming South American genus *Trichocereus*, most forms of which are robust shrubby to columnar versions of *echinopsis*, Easter lily cacti. Here for the first time I saw trichocereus hybrids made by noted Santa Barbara plantsman, Frank Reinelt. These hybrids are in their element in coastal Santa Barbara, for they form tight, sculpted clusters and their creamy white, yellow, orange, and red-flaring trumpet-shaped flowers often stay open during the day. The best cactus in the garden is a huge saguaro-like, branched specimen of *Trichocereus terscheckii*, native to Bolivia and Argentina. It is similar to the equally massive *T. pasacana*, common in the Huntington, but has fewer spines. Another trichocereus, possibly a very rare South American species, is upright like a gaggle of curious Al Capp schmoos. It stands out beautifully among the New Zealand flax and comes alive in the spring with large, bright yellow blossoms.

It is refreshing to see many shrubby prickly pear cacti in the garden. They tend to be unpopular in collectors' gardens because of their reputation as space eaters. However, they can be found where there is room and lots of sun, as evidenced by the huge cow's tongue from Texas, which commands a berm for itself. If not cut back occasionally, it will form a defiant fortress twenty to thirty feet across. Frank admires it because the newly opened blossoms are bright yellow then after a couple of days turn orange, thus putting on a floral display in two colors. This is one of the worst opuntias for glochids, the clusters of readily detached short barbed spinelets that are one of the primary reasons people hate cacti. They are found exclusively on opuntias, and Luther Burbank made a lot of money claiming he developed a spineless cactus that cattle would eat. However, his spineless opuntias did have highly irritating glochids; some reverted to spiney forms, and for the most part the cattle ate them only in times of extreme hardship.

Ganna Walska Lotusland, Montecito

Lotusland is the floristic testament to the spiritual quest of famed, sometimes notorious, opera star Madame Ganna Walska. It is one of the strangest, yet most enchanting gardens to behold. Its cactus and succulent gardens and plantings at her Montecito subtropical estate are eccentric, almost disturbing. Were the gardens her personal opera favorites arranged for large botanical orchestras? Or maybe sarcastic evaluations of the inner lives of her six husbands? These gardens do tell a story, but not of a tortured soul seeking horticultural solace. Madame Walska was flamboyant, demanding, angry, and very driven to push garden design to realms that have never been revisited. Biographies and commentaries seem preoccupied with the influential men in her life, who practically stood in line to marry her. With her robust resources, she supported many of those men, then finally replaced them all, making flowers the objects of her eros. At that time, and for a period of time thereafter, she became designer, construction superviser, and head gardener for her thirty-seven-acre estate. Ganna Walska was drawn to Eastern spiritualism as well as to flowers, shrubs, and trees. The direction of her quest would have made her an excellent candidate for analysis with Carl Jung but she was less interested in inner acts of introspection or elevated consciousness than in outer acts of gardening. This required hoes, rakes, and shovels, an army of horticultural advisers and gardeners, and tons of plants gathered throughout the Southwest.

Ganna Walska purchased her Montecito estate in 1941. It had an interesting past, some elements of which are still alive in the garden. Originally it belonged to the early Santa Barbara resident R. Kinton Stevens, who began a tropical and subtropical nursery there in 1882. The following year he issued the first tropical and subtropical plant catalogue in California. The Chilean wine palm, the dragon's blood tree, and the Monterey cypress are reminders of the bygone era of Santa Barbara's early horticultural pioneers. The property changed hands many times, but one important owner, E.P. Gavit, demolished the house and built his own in the Mediterranean style and named it La Cuesta Linda. Peter Riedel, a garden designer and associate of Dr. Franceschi, laid out the

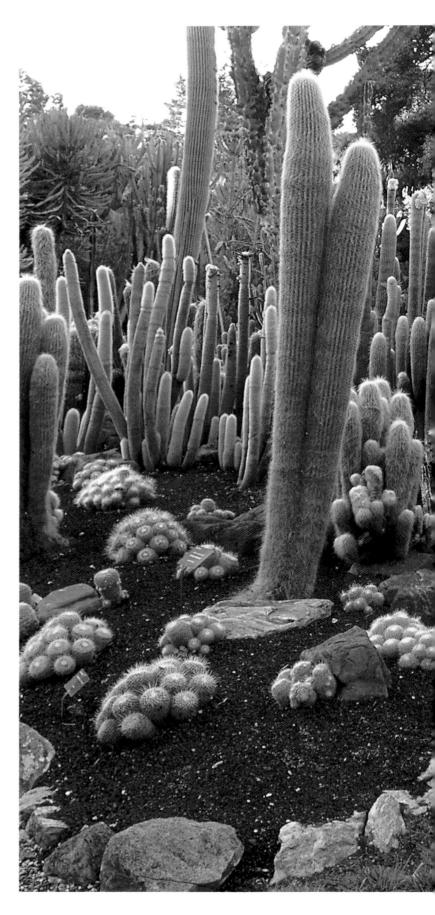

Display of fuzzy white-spined cacti (left);
far right, columnar *trichocereus* and
golden barrels.

Torch cactus (*Cleistocactu strausii*) and cleistogamous flowers.

gardens, assisted by R. Kinton Stevens's son. It is not known if any of their plantings survive. La Cuesta Linda was much illustrated in Winifrid Dobyn's 1931 publication *California Gardens*. The house was renamed Tibetland by its new owner, Ganna Walska, in a hapless effort to accommodate a lover. By 1946, manless, she renamed it Lotusland.

Most of the garden scenes illustrated in Dobyn's book were replaced, not systematically, but as Ganna Walska's visionary implulse dictated. She enlisted the help of Santa Barbara garden designers Lockwood de Forest and Ralph Stevens, who were primarily responsible for laying out the formal aspects of the gardens, establishing lines of sight, and especially acquiring the endless inventory of exotic, weird, least-known, and only known specimens of whatever plant or plants resonated with her botanical fantasies. Thematically, the estate was divided into a series of themes or features, and for our purposes, we will mention only those connected to succulent plants.

Cacti and succulents were Ganna Walska's passion, but this passion did not crystallize until the early 1950s. She purchased them by the hundreds, much in the spirit of William Hertrich and the Huntington Desert Garden, the exeption being that she had an incredible eye for form, color, and texture. What she needed, but did not have, was a railroad. She was intrigued by rarity, but her trophies had to have eye appeal. She did not purchase collections, however, just specimens that would make sensational displays in her designs. As you wander through her maze of gardens, not knowing what to expect at each turn of the path, your eye is challenged by her idiosyncratic combinations—all in good taste. The most conspicuous display is along the original entry drive and west side of the residence. The pink stuccoed building energizes her mostly intact displays of cacti and euphorbias. The much photographed *Euphorbia ammak* (sometimes referred to as *E. ingens*) with its agonizingly contorted stems that droop and even creep on to the drive look like they are desperately searching for the nearest exit. This plant always amazes me because of its anomalous growth form. Early photos show a typical tree euphorbia with upright scaffolding—what did she do to it? Like a Puccini opera, it started high and ended low.

Across from the house, now the office and headquarters of Ganna Walska Lotusland and the Lotusland Foundation, is a remnant of Kinton Stevens's dragon's blood tree display. The trees are planted so close together that the effect is both eerie and mysterious. Dragon's blood trees grow slowly and so only now is it becoming apparent that they were planted too closely—for their broad umbrella-like crowns are knitting into a large mass of stubby branches. A full-grown *Dracaena draco* has a trunk diameter of twelve to twenty-two feet. At some point something needs to be done about the crowding: box and move, or chop and toss.

Along the paved drive armed legions of golden barrel cacti are set out for review and looked over by huge, healthy specimens of night-blooming cereus. Across the drive are platoons of Brazilian lemon ball cactus (*Notocactus leninghausii*) growing in massive clumps. In April and May, spectacular yellow blooms cover the tops of the plants. In the background are colonnades of densely planted blue fuzzies—hairy, woolly columnar cacti native to Brazil and Mexico. Their powder blue stems and soft downy white wool makes them look good enough to pet. Do it and you get a handful of sharp spines! You just cannot trust cacti. A corps of gardeners work to keep the displays within the design concepts laid down by Ganna Walska. The plantings are immaculate and well groomed. The gardener-horticulturists say problems with soil and drainage have taken their toll, but soil renovation in the cactus gardens has improved drainage in the clayey soil. There are plans to map the collection and develop a labeling system. In spite of Ganna Walska's aspirations, a garden of this size and diversity becomes more than an artistically designed garden. It is also a collection, and collection management, labeling, and mapping have become important

Scenic vista looking across to blue garden.

Overleaf: Tour de force cactuscape with
Ganna Walska's house.

Beneath the dragon's blood trees (*Dracaena draco*) showing dichotomous branching.

Young Pony Tail Palms (*Beaucarnea recurvata*) from Mexico.

challenges for staff. One innovation often difficult and costly to achieve is biological pest control. An acre or more of ground is set aside behind the scenes for cultivation of host plants that support a beneficial army of insects which feed on damaging pests such as mealy bug and scale, the nemeses of cactus growers everywhere.

Lotusland's roots reach back to the 1880s, the Golden Age of Horticulture, which means any surviving trees are enormous. Historic specimens of eucalyptus, Monterey pine, and palm have increased their reach to where once-sunny gardens are now shaded. This creates problems for sun-loving aloes and cacti; conserving the succulents means making tough decisions about trees.

The Aloe Garden was renovated and many new species added in the 1970s when Ganna Walska realized that she could no longer micromanage all plant-maintenance routines and hired Charles Glass and Robert Foster, formerly editors of the *Journal of the Cactus and Succulent Society of America*, to manage and renovate her gardens. Their major achievement, in addition to sustaining an amicable relationship with the Madame, was creation of the Cycad Garden, today recognized as one of the finest displays of these fossil plants in the country. Glass and Foster initiated many of the restoration projects in the 1970s, particularly in areas landscaped with succulents and bromeliads. During renovation of the Aloe Garden, much of the old soil was replaced and the aloes replanted. However, the garden looks tired and partly overgrown. The *Aloe dichotoma* and *A. ramosissima* specimens that were sensational years ago are nearly gone (one or two remain); the associated whimsical clamshell, abalone, and coral motif remains but is no longer anchored to the smooth-trunked aloes. The original concept was to create a succulent sunken garden with a choncological underwater effect; but part of the problem is lack of light. The aloes are surrounded by several centenarian Chilean wine palms over forty feet tall and with massive trunks up to five feet in diameter, and by enormous eucalyptus trees that all but block out the afternoon light. The most successful aloe planting among over one hundred species is *A. brevifolia*, a greenish-grayish leaved mound-forming species from the Cape. It performs beautifully, making tight, compact clumps that

Queen Victoria agaves (*Agave victoriae reginae*) nearly full grown.

spill dramatically over the red crushed volcanic rock mulch. The flowers are orange and borne on short spikes. It is one of the best plantings in the garden.

The use of rock mulch is controversial. It may be satisfactory in a formal or more designed garden, such as Lotusland and the Getty Center, but if overused may contradict a more desired natural look. It is a useful moisture-retention aid—not always a desirable feature in a desert garden of limited light and less-than-perfect drainage. It should be added that mulch has a slight deterrent effect on weeds and is a deterrent to germinating broadcast wildflower seed.

Near the Blue Garden is a garden of soft succulents, possibly planted in the 1970s or more recently. It features *echeveria*, *aeonium*, *kalanchoe*, and *sedum*—all in the crassula family, which all complement one another in their soft pastel tones and smooth leaves. The Blue Garden should not be overlooked, for here one finds masses of blue kleinia (*Senecio mandraliscae*) accented by the broad grayish leaved and sculpturesque *Agave franzosinii*, one of the most garden-worthy agaves for the spacious gardens and one that has been cultivated for years in Mediterranean gardens. Howard Scott Gentry, the great agave authority and devotee of Mayahuel, the goddess of

Shaded succulent garden: in the foreground,
Black Aeonium (*Aeonium arboreum*
'Zwartkop'); left: *Senecio tomentosa*.

pulque, once remarked that this species has never been found in the wild, which may suggest a cultivated origin.

The chief executive gardener, as Ganna Walska termed herself, died in 1984, but before she did she created the Lotusland Foundation in order to preserve her unique garden and to maintain it as a horticultural reserve for the study of ornamental plants. Today the garden is open to guided tours by reservation only. The Lotusland Foundation's mission statement acknowledges the garden's value in promoting *ex situ* conservation: "To preserve and enhance the spectacular collections of exotic plants on the Montecito estate of the late Madame Ganna Walska, and through

interpretations of these collections to foster increased knowledge and appreciation of the importance of plants and the need for their conservation." There should be an added corollary: "To continue Ganna Walska's spiritual quest for the Green Man and reverence for the vegetable spirit in the context of the imagery of garden design."

What I find most lacking when I visit Lotusland is Madame Ganna Walska herself. The garden experience, the botanical stage, really is incomplete without its star performer. This shrine to her extraverted spiritual quest was designed for her own pure and personal pleasure. I would have chased her, too!

Aloe garden. Foreground: *Aloe brevifolia* clumps; right: flowering Fan Aloe (*A. plicatilis*).

Unique (relaxed) specimen of *Euphorbia ingens* growing next to the house.

Gary Lyons Garden, Burbank

It is difficult to describe this garden because it is mine; I look at it every day. I started my cactus garden when I was twelve and we grew up together. Perhaps that is why it is somewhat embarrassing to talk about it. It is like going through boxes of comics and toys. Most of the time I do not think much about the garden as a landscape; I am too busy weeding, watering, and getting rid of bugs. This obsession with cacti began when a friend gave me a potted Easter lily cactus. Its baseball shape, numerous low ribs, and very short spines somehow made it irresistible and I thought it would do better if planted in the ground. My aunt saw a budding horticulturist and gave me succulents from her garden, originally planted by my grandparents. I was hooked, and that began the gradual transformation of my parents' yard to a desert botanical garden. It was a garden of whatever I could find; my rock collection became the foundation of the rockwork. Other, more suitable rocks were added through the years, but that collection of bits and pieces of malachite, uranium ore, gold ore, pyrite, obsidian, and howlite peek out here and there. In terms of design the rockwork does not make sense, but to me the rocks are just old friends whom I greet each day.

As my interest grew, so did the number of plants. I joined the Cactus and Succulent Society of America, which met at the Pasadena Public Library, and there I met many of the great names in the cactus world. I remember meeting Professor Lyman Benson of Pomona College, the foremost authority on cacti of the United States and Canada; Harry Johnson, owner of Johnson's Cactus Gardens, originator of the Paramount Hybrids; Howard Gates, pioneer explorer of Baja California; and Scott Haselton, editor of the *Journal of the Cactus and Succulent Society of America*. I spent all my money on cacti at Johnson's nursery, then the largest retail cactus nursery in Southern California. Many of my cactus books were purchased at Scott Haselton's Abbey Garden Press on Union Street, which is now part of Pasadena's Old Town.

My garden is an unfinished collage of smaller flowering cacti, aloes, euphorbias, mesembs, and whatever else I find interesting and want to look at in my limited space, for no gardener's garden is ever finished. I have room for a few small hechtias and calibanus. Some of my favorites are two species of bottle palm, a dragon's blood tree, and the ocotillo-like palo adan (*Fouquieria macdougallii*). I grew each from seed over twenty-five years ago and they are now full grown and flowering. The palo adan is especially attractive with long whip-like stems and bouquets of bright red flowers—a great attraction for hummingbirds. There is a collection of medicinal aloes—I am doing historical research on *Aloe vera* and am constantly on the lookout for variant plants. Small, globular cacti are my favorites, but I grow most in pots. I prefer the old clay pots because they reduce the possibility of root rot setting in during wet winters. Eventually, an exceptional specimen will become large enough to be featured someplace in the garden. One of the so-called chin cacti (*Gymnocalycium horstii*) is so well adapted it can be grown in the ground. However, I usually decide to keep them and the pincushion cacti in pots.

Much of the garden is locked in a life-and-death struggle with a neighbor's pecan tree. Near the tree I plant aloes, gasterias, and haworthias because they tolerate shade and invasive roots. The tree is so invasive it even invades my sense of well being, especially when the roots go right up the drainage holes in the pots. In order to stay ahead of the tree, extra water, fertilizer, and vigilance are required. However, the most unforgiving aspect of the pecan is its messiness. I have spent hundreds of hours surgically removing the tens of thousands of catkins it drops each spring, the pounds of pecans that fall each autumn (assisted by squirrels and flocks of crows—and a parrot or two), and the tons of leaves that drift down each November. Sometimes I get fed up and cover half the garden with shade cloth to catch the debris. Several times each

Foreground: flowering *Euphorbia fruticosa* from Yemen; background: *Agave* aff. *titanota*.

Overleaf: Garden scene showing reticulated trunk of twenty eight year old *Beaucarnea stricta*.

Portion of prickly herbaceous border.

Left foreground: Agave aff. *titanota*; bottom: Lemon Ball (*Notocactus leninghausii*); background: *N. magnificus*; top left: potted Milk Barrel.

year, I wander through the garden and—like the Little Prince in Saint-Exupéry's novel, who digs out invasive baobab trees on his tiny asteroid—grub hundreds of germinating pecan seedlings carefully planted by the squirrels.

I fertilize, using Miracle Gro and occasionally a triple sixteen granular fertilizer, three or four times a year. Some of my special plants get servings of slow-release Osmocote. Watering is not to any set schedule; I learned years ago from Harry Johnson that you let the soil dry out between waterings. Not doing so invites root and stem rot, plus a myriad of surface fungi. Cacti, more than crassulaceous succulents, prefer to dry out between waterings. I reserve watering for sunny mornings, even if it means waiting. This dictum applies to all succulents in the garden. Once in awhile I check to see that the water is getting to the roots and just hope it does not rain the next day.

There is some coherence to my garden. Next to the driveway is my Prickly Herbaceous Border (eat your heart out

Gertrude Jekyll). It consists of small agaves, aloes, borzicactus, and trichocereus. The garden is not all spine. A border is interplanted with blue-flowered statice (*Limonium perezii*). My summer tour de force is the Mexican bird of paradise (*Caesalpinia mexicana*) with its masses of fiery, bright red-orange blossoms. If cut back in the fall, it makes a beautiful shrub for small spaces.

In sunny parts of the garden, I grow agave, medium-sized aloes, more statice, and pink evening primrose. These, plus plantings of autumn sage (*Salvia greggii*), complement the sturdy white-variegated century plants (*Agave americana* var. *mediopicta* 'Alba') not to mention providing a colorful spring show. On the south side, away from the pecan and where there is more sun, I have golden barrels, several species of yellow-flowering Brazilian notocactus, and numerous pincushion cacti. There is a small rockery that slowly evolved in the sunnier south-facing backyard and where I planted smaller cacti. The showiest are the Brasilian *Notocactus magnificus*, so called because of symmetrical ribs, golden yellow spines, and absolutely brilliant flowers.

Garden scene; center: potted Chin Cactus
(*Gymnocalycium horstii*); upper left: *Agave ocahui.*

Some small agaves do well here. My favorite is *Agave ocahui*, which forms a single rosette of more than a hundred straight, dark green leaves. From a distance it looks like a ball. Since it has no offsets, it dies after shooting up a tall column of thousands of pale yellow flowers. The single-stemmed, or monocarpic, agaves I like in the garden are reinforced by potted backup plants.

A prickly dwarf terrestrial bromeliad from Argentina called *abromeitiella* oozes like moss over the stones beneath a large bottle palm. The little bromeliad eventually has to be moved because it is growing like a glacier, right onto the path and heading straight for the next bed. This is one of the many new bromeliad species first grown outdoors in Southern California at the Huntington. One of the Huntington programs is to test new or untried plants in gardens. A few get the test of fire in my own garden. In this way, I discovered that the *abromeitiella* does not take hot afternoon sun, so it needs shade. At home and at the Huntington, I often research a new plant by looking up its description, finding out where it is native, and hopefully getting an idea how it might best be grown.

I am accustomed to moving some of the cacti as the sun progresses through the seasons. The sunniest place is reserved for the small Chihuahuan Desert cacti from Texas and Mexico. These include such genera as *astrophytum*, *coryphantha*, *echinocereus*, *ferocactus*, *mammillaria*, and *thelocactus*. Because I fear the effect of the winter rains, I like to keep them in clay pots. These are seedlings, mostly purchased from nurseries in Arizona. If there is too much rain, I cover them with plastic sheeting. Since they get overhead and afternoon sun, in summer I often cover them with shade cloth to prevent sunburn. It is surprising to see that so many cacti do not tolerate strong hot sun. The reason is that many cacti grow in the wild in the protective shade of such nurse plants as creosote and mesquite, not to mention the protective shelter of rocky crevices. The more one learns about habitat the more one understands the reasons for that lack of tolerance. Most deserts where cacti grow in summer experience higher humidity in that season; some, such as the Sonoran Desert have what is called the summer monsoon, so along with the heat comes high humidity. The high atmosperic moisture level has the effect of dispersing sunlight, something that does not occur in the bone-dry summer heat waves of Southern California. Another factor affecting sun tolerance in cacti is the number of on and off days we experience in Southern California; that is, the hazy overcast days that can last for weeks, followed by what we call Santa Ana conditions, where the temperature is very high and the humidity dangerously low. The Chihuahuan Desert, primarily southwest Texas and north central Mexico, is one of the cooler deserts in winter and plants from there are least likely to be affected by our rare frosts.

My haworthias look best in partial shade, but not in the ground. I keep them, as well as a collection of hundreds of African succulents, including miniature aloe hybrids and rare thick-trunk (*pachycaul*) succulents, in pots on benches where there is partial shade. I spend hours, often in evenings, fussing over them: removing dead leaves and flower stalks and patroling for snails and slugs, which love to munch the flowers and growth tips. Snails and slugs go after echeverias and pachyphytums and nibble their way through the fresh growth of everthing but the toxic euphorbias.

Most of the plants in my garden that are in the ground I regard as survivors; they are scarred from battles with sun or cold, or from not enough room. To me the beat-up look gives them the character one would encounter in the wild. I must confess I get somewhat bored looking at plants grown to spotless perfection and exhibited at cactus shows. Granted, they are impressive accomplishments, but their appearance reflects an obsession with perfection, not gardening, and are often unrecognizable as the forms found in the wild.

Most of my life has been spent in my garden or in making someone else's cactus garden. One of my earliest memories is a dream of being in a beautifully planted garden. My garden in Burbank and those I created for others sustain me with the knowledge that their designs came from efforts to give voice to something deep within me. I still don't understand it. If it were not for these desert gardens, I would not be here.

Fick Garden, Pasadena

The Fick's garden reflects a gentler, kinder love of succulents, one connected with the need to maintain livable outdoor space to complement their Craftsman home located in the historic Pasadena Arroyo. The origin of the garden is of interest because it was very much influenced by the nearby Huntington Desert Garden.

One summer many years ago, Virginia and Otto Fick's daughter had a summer job at the Huntington, making plant labels in the library basement. Understandably, Amy found the job tedious and communicated to me her desire to work in the Desert Garden. There was an opening, and so she spent the rest of the summer planting and watering cacti. From time to time I gave her cuttings of succulents to take home and grow in her garden. In turn, she gave them to her mother, Virginia, who planted them among her other plants. Before long, Virginia volunteered for garden work, grooming plantings of succulents. She also became a regular at Huntington plant sales. Her numerous acquisitions of cacti and succulents soon overwhelmed her garden of herbaceous perennials; however, she found a common ground for non-succulent and succulent coexistence. The result is not so much designed composition as an artistic creation that reflects the hand of the caring gardener.

The Fick's succulent garden is concentrated in the front yard, spilling onto the parkway. A thirty-foot thorny bottle-trunked floss silk tree (*Chorisia speciosa*) is Virginia's pride and joy. It is planted in a strip next to the street and was a month-old seedling from the Huntington that I had given Amy. The floss silk tree is from Brazil and Argentina and is related to the kapok tree (*ceiba*). It is a popular and colorful landscape tree in general use in Southern California. Its large, showy pink flowers appear in masses, usually when the tree is deciduous. It is probably bat pollinated, and when the seed pods split open out float bits of white fluff, each containing a large black seed. The fluff is used for stuffing pillows.

There are many contrasts in this small garden, some unexpected. For example, in February, a thorny pyracantha is afire

Composition of low growing succulents and tall cacti and euphorbias. Note potted Burro Tail (*Sedum morganianum*).

with bright red berries, forming an unusual and intense backdrop to plantings of *agave*, *aeonium*, *crassula*, and lemon ball cactus. The small patch of grass is surrounded by bedded-out displays of *Aeonium* 'Zwartkop' complemented by pale fleshy tones from a large planting of *Graptopetalum paraguayense*. There are some odd but workable combinations of ornamental oxalis, candy tuft, and the creeping blue kleinia (*Senecio mandraliscae*).

The cacti Virginia brings into the picture are not particularly vicious; for example, *Cereus hildmannianus*, a night-blooming cereus—bat and moth pollinated as all cerei are—features very short spines and a soft, smooth-textured surface. Other examples are a golden cascading pot of *Hildewintera aureispina* and a fuzzy torch cactus, *Cleistocactus strausii*.

Virginia is very proud of her garden, as well she should be, and is especially keen to work with succulents as expressions of texture and color. She does not concern herself with names, regrettably a characteristic of most gardeners, in contrast to the maniacal collector. She just enjoys the year-round show.

Other displays of interest in the Fick garden include the South Africa cow's horn euphorbia (*Euphorbia grandicornis*), with its exaggerated spine pairs (actually, modified leaf stipules), and a well-tended specimen of a sprawling cereoid cactus from Mexico known only as *Nyctocereus serpentinus*, once common in gardens but now becoming rare. These are unlikely juxtapositions as they are interplanted with cylindrical opuntias, sprawling variegated elephant bush (*Portulacaria afra* 'Variegated'), bedding crassulas such as *Crassula erosula*, and *Cotyledon orbiculata*. Yet they create a successful composition, perhaps for no other reason than Virginia's determination to make them succeed and some help from the old Craftsman rock planters and terraces.

Unlikely combinations that work because a
devoted gardener makes them so.

Overleaf: A sunny corner showing a mix of potted and planted
specimens; note the traditional smooth granite border.

Los Angeles City Zoo, Griffith Park, Los Angeles

The eighty-acre Los Angeles City Zoo is home to two hundred species of cacti and succulents that are found in animal exhibits and specially laid out landscapes to complement the exotic tone of the grounds. The extensive use of succulents was the idea of Dr. Warren Thomas, zoo director from 1965 to 1991. He visited the Huntington Desert Garden, got ideas, and then plants. The Huntington and many other public and private gardens have long-established traditions of exchanging and donating plant materials; this generosity saves countless cuttings of succulents and unwanted plants from the compost heap. Some of the plants donated to the zoo were planted in animal exhibits—a real learning experience because most were eaten or trampled. The remainder were planted in scenic islands and ultimately became specialized displays.

The Zoo's landscape exemplifies the city's historic adherence to the subtropical paradise image that brought millions of people to fill the orchards, farms, ranches, and nurseries of Southern California with tract homes. The image is still doing its job as each year over one million children and adults pass through the zoo's turnstyles. Throughout the hilly terrain, visitors are drawn in to exhibits to view rare and endangered animals, and by mood-setting plants. In the 1970s the concept of zoo horticulture gained momentum, and greater interest in plants strongly affected how zoos were perceived by the public. Years ago if plants were used in or around animal exhibits, it was to provide modest staging. The zoo had barely opened its doors to the public when the concept of animal exhibit design began a transformation that acknowledged the relevance of plant biodiversity and natural habitat to animal survival. In short, a realistic and naturalistic concept of animal habitat became the basis for displaying animals.

The zoo desert gardens, consisting mostly of small islands dispersed throughout the zoo, reflect the Huntington Desert Garden's influence as an important source of propagating material. The very rare blue form of Agave parryi var. *truncata* thrives and flowers in the cactus garden where it can be enjoyed both by the public and gorillas. The zoo has numerous specimens of a tree-like prickly pear cactus (*Opuntia streptacantha*) from Mexico, where it

Hedgehog cacti from the southwest:
Arizona Rainbow (*Echinocereus pectinatus*
var. *rigidissimus*); right *E. dasyacanthus*.

is used as a folk remedy to treat type II diabetes and now demonstrated to produce compounds that lower blood sugar. The dragon's blood tree (*Dracaena draco*) from the Canary Islands, known for its astringent resin used in pharmacy, was imported to Europe in earlier times. The resin was also used to stain wood and marble. Seventeenth-century Italian violinmakers used dragon's blood as a wood stain, and some scholars think it contributed to the incomparable sound of the Stradivarius violin. Now there may be fewer than twenty-five dragon's blood trees growing wild in the Canaries. Its preservation is afforded by its popularity as a cultivated exotic in Mediterranean-climate gardens.

The Baja Bed is the visitor's first encounter with zoo succulents. Except for the enormous bottle palm from mainland Mexico, it is planted with succulents from Lower, or Baja, California. Here we see thick-trunk succulents such as copal (*Bursera microphylla*), which belongs to the frankincense family. Copal resin was used for incense in the mission era. There is also the powdery white-chalk plant known as siempreviva (*Dudleya brittonii*) and the Persian slipper (*Pedilanthus macrocarpus*), a crested euphorbia

relative that fascinates children and adults alike with its cockscomb stems and red flowers that look like little slippers. Succulent euphorbias are uncommon in the Western Hemisphere, but the scraggly *Euphorbia xantii* upstages all African milkweeds. Badly in need of a common name, this euphorb in spring disappears beneath billowy masses of crimson flowers that fade to pale pink, exploding in color like no other euphorbia. It needs lots of sunny space in the home garden and is best used either for accent or background effect. I have never understood why it took so long to appear in cultivation. Even today, despite of repeated offerings at Huntington plant sales, it remains uncommon.

The North American garden contrasts with the adjacent gorilla compound. The huge male silverback gazes from his high perch and daily surveys the cacti. This is the first cactus garden planted, and in the dense thickets of succulents is the pink-flowered cane cholla (*Opuntia imbricata*). Chollas are the plants that make people hate cacti. Sometimes short stems, called joints, readily attach themselves to whatever and whomever touches them. This is called vegetative dispersal, and the means of transport

Use of agaves in the landscape; on the right, *Agave americana* 'Picta.'

is facilitated by near-microscopic reverse barbs mounted on very sharp spines, thus permitting the detached joint to be firmly and painfully planted in the skin. The ensuing effort to shake off the joint just makes matters worse; sometimes these joints (and their spines) have to be yanked out of the flesh with pliers. Ironically, chollas are standard landscape items in our Southwest deserts. As a security plant, chollas do the job too well; but some species of cane cholla are tolerable and decorative when kept out of reach in sunny and well-drained areas.

While I was a landscape gardener at the zoo I designed a cactus garden (now gone to make way for the new orangutan exhibit) for succulents native to Mexico. Thankfully the red volcanic rock overused at the Huntington was not available. Instead we used a brown sandstone found in Griffith Park. However, the effect worked well with the cacti, and received positive comment from the public. There was one very big problem. This garden was just a few feet from the habitat of Sampson, the largest male African elephant in North America. He did not like anything on two legs and had the annoying habit of attracting viewers to the edge of his

Use of soft and hard succulents as barrier;
center: South African *Crassula arborescens*.

compound then hosing them with a trunkful of water followed by salvos of fecal matter. Planting this garden was an unforgettable experience. It could be done only by keeping one's back to Sampson: he never missed an opportunity to hit a moving target (and was a good shot) with chunks of flying feces. Few gardens succeed in the presence of hostile pachyderms.

There have been efforts to incorporate plants, including succulents, into exhibits. Many of these projects came to grief after observations of how captive animals treat plants materials in their exhibits. For instance, no one had any idea that a coyote would eat a large century plant, the prairie dog devour rare specimen yuccas, or the meerkats bury the aloes. Common sense dictated zero plantings for large hoofstock, but corps of animal observers have gathered much needed information on how captive animals treat plants. One of the goals of zoo horticulture is to observe plant-animal compatibility, to keep records of toxic plants and see they are not used in exhibit design, and to learn what plants may be useful as browse.

Many of the succulents in the zoo form the nucleus of yet-to-be-developed economic and medicinal plant displays. Pulque is not exactly medicine; rather, it is a beer-like beverage popular, perhaps since ancient times, in Mexico and Central America. Pulque is the fermented juice of the largest agaves, such as *Agave tecta* from Guatemala and *A. mapisaga var. lisa* from the Mexico highlands. These agaves were probably the result of centuries of selection of the best pulque-producing plants. The larger the plant, the more juice (*aguamiel*) produced. A single plant can yield, for a year or more, up to one hundred liters of aguamiel, which is scooped out of the plant and fermented for several days before being consumed.

Succulents are an untapped educational resource for economic and medicinal plant displays. The zoo is expanding its concept of sensitizing the public to the complexities and value of the natural world, and its master plan gives greater visibility to the botanical world.

Unfortunately, the zoo master plan calls for removal of most, if not all, the theme succulent gardens in order to create rain forest biomes. There are plans to relocate the plants to temporary quarters, eventually including them in desert biomes that will include nonsucculents. At least the plants will survive, including the endangered dragon's blood tree, for there will be a Canary Island bed that will draw attention to the role of zoos and other public spaces as settings for *ex situ* conservation programs. I am a bit concerned about this tendency to construct rainforest biomes at the expense of dryland and desert biomes. It will undoubtedly increase gate receipts, but is it sends a skewed conservation message to the children of Los Angeles, whose heritage of botanical diversity has been nearly clear cut by developers. Although forest destruction and the destruction of exotic species is something schoolchildren should know and worry about, in reality they can do far less for the rainforest than they can for their home grounds. Rather, they be should be taught to be concerned about the destruction of the complex Southern California ecosystems, which, as citizens and eventual decision makers they can affect. What they learn will eventually determine how they design and live in Southern California.

The horticulture and botanical program of the Los Angeles City Zoo is just beginning; the staff is in the process of creating gardens and programs that will show the public how plants and animals survive by mutualistic strategies—such as flowers and their pollinators, fruit and seed and their dispersers—and what strategies they adopt for protection and survival. Also to be addressed is the increasing awareness that that for biological survival anywhere in the world, humans have to be factored in to wildlife conservation issues. Therefore, the new education program will include educational gardens to consist of more than the present browse garden; there will be new gardens of rare and endangered plants, displays of food plants consumed by peoples of many different societies, and displays of medicinal and economic plants. There also are plans for hummingbird and butterfly gardens. Such displays will give a plant-oriented dimension to the zoo's successful school programs.

Teresa Proscewicz, the zoo grounds and gardens superintendent, welcomes these new and innovative programs; actually, many of them are her own ideas, and she hopes someday the zoo will be renamed the Los Angeles Zoo and Botanical Garden. It is difficult to believe a city the size of Los Angeles, with the great plant diversity in its city parks, has no horticulturist or botanist. Perhaps more incredible is the fact that it has no botanic garden. In another time, Elysian Park near Dodger Stadium was a botanic garden, planted in the 1880s. According to Teresa Proscewicz, there has not been a city horticulturist since the 1950s. Griffith and Elysian parks alone probably have more botanical diversity than any other park system in the country. From the botanical perspective, the zoo now has a mission to create and maintain a world-class botanic garden. Plants are now presented, as they are in many zoos, simply as background staging for animal display. The zoo of the future should be designed in such a manner that equal importance is given to animals and plants. This presents the strongest conservation message to the public.

Rancho Santa Ana Botanic Garden, Claremont

Rancho Santa Ana Botanic Garden (RSABG) was created in 1927 by Suzanna Bixby Bryant, a highly educated and successful landowner in Southern California. Her father owned the 6,000-acre Rancho Santa Ana, in the Puente Hills of Orange County near Yorba Linda and a bit north of the R.J. O'Neill Ranch. She was associated with another ranch through marriage to John W. Bixby, owner of Rancho Los Alamitos, in what is now Long Beach. Susanna Bixby Bryant lived at Rancho Santa Ana. Her residential grounds were laid out by Frederick Law Olmsted, Jr., of the Olmstead Brothers. While their father is best known for the design of Central Park in New York, the sons are perhaps best known in Southern California for the Palos Verdes Estates.

When she decided to convert 200 acres of ranchland to a botanic garden, she sought assistance from California's finest horticulturists and garden designers, such as Ernest Braunton, Beatrix Farrand, Theodore Payne, and Ralph Dalton Cornell. Like Henry Huntington, she knew what she wanted and would search and search until she found the person or persons who would work with her to create not just a garden or an ersatz botanic garden, but California's most prestigious botanic garden, dedicated exclusively to the cultivation of California's then little-known native plants. Unlike Huntington, she was acquainted personally with America's finest botanists: Charles Sprague Sargent, Willis Linn Jepson, Alice Eastwood, LeRoy Abrams, and even America's greatest horticulturist, Liberty Hyde Bailey. All were consulted in the conceptualizing, planning, construction of what was eventually known as the Rancho Santa Ana Botanic Garden.

Tragically, Mrs. Bryant died suddenly in 1946 and it was decided that her botanic garden, herbarium, and library might better serve botanical science and horticulture if it had a closer association to a college. Phillip Munz, the garden's first director and author of *A California Flora*, taught at Pomona College like so many of Bryant's original professional staff; certainly one motivation was to close the distance between the college and the botanic garden. Between 1950 and 1952, thousands of plants were moved to the present eighty-six-acre site just above the Claremont Colleges. Many plants were left behind and survived until most of the land was subdivided.

One of RSABG's primary goals at Claremont is to develop and introduce cultivars for the nursery trade and home gardener. This was part of the original program under Munz, and over the years at least seventy-five named cultivars and selections have been

71

Six foot inflorescence of *Nolina parryi* ssp. *wolfii*.
Background: California Juniper (*Juniperus californica*).

developed at the garden's growing facilities. In 1971, RSABG became the first botanic garden in California to patent a plant selection, the popular *Mahonia* 'Golden Abundance.' Cultivar development and introduction is a much-needed program to advance the cause of native plant gardening; many species are difficult to grow in the subtropical landscape and maintenance regime, where soils are heavily amended and watered throughout the year. Many shrubs, such as ceanothus and manzanita, and trees, such as the California buckeye (*Aesculus californica*) and the decorative madrone (*Arbutus menziesi*), are adapted to summer drought. The Rancho Santa Ana Botanic Garden has become an education center devoted to informing the public as to the value of water conservation and how best to landscape with native plants. Their goal of conserving the California native flora is furthered through numerous symposia, publications, classes, and public field trips. As part of an academic institution, the garden, especially the plant communities area, is an important resource as a living reference library for the various botanical programs offered by the Claremont Colleges graduate school.

Most of the cacti and other succulents belong to the Mojavean and Sonoran Provinces. Bart O'Brien, RSABG director of horticulture, says there are plans to develop an improved Mojave Desert Province. Sonoran Floristic Regime at RSABG is a collective term for all the deserts in California, except the Great Basin Desert, elements of which extend to the eastern Sierra. We cactus nuts stick to the concept of at least two deserts—Mojavean and Sonoran—in Southern California, each broken down into subsections. For example, the Mojave Desert is in the northeast portion of Southern California with upper and lower Mojave deserts, and the Sonoran Desert is in the southeast portion of Southern California. The southern desert can be divided in to what is called the Arizona Sonoran Desert and the Colorado Desert. Arguments over where the various desert boundaries are located swirl around what plant or plants characterize each desert, such as the Joshua tree indicating the Mojave Desert.

The eighty-five acre botanic garden includes a formal landscape on what is called Indian Hill Mesa, which emphasizes landscaping and plants suitable for the residential garden and includes the new and spectacular California Cultivar Garden, where the best of RSABG's numerous cultivars and hybrids are put on display in several raised beds. Bart O'Brien says succulents do not work that well in the demonstration beds, so they have their own display, which emphasizes the desert-adapted siempreviva or chalk plant (*Dudleya brittonii*) and the spineless totem pole cactus (*Lophocereus schotti* 'Monstrose')—Baja California natives.

Strangely, cactophobia permeates garden thinking in Southern California. The disinterest in using cacti and succulents in both landscaping and fire control is laughable in light of the popularity of cacti in Southwest desert landscaping and the popularity of succulents in gardens during Southern California's Golden Age of Horticulture. One hopes this attitude will change when firescaping and gardening with drought-tolerant plants gain more acceptance in professional circles. However, RSABG does display a number of new and garden-adapted herbaceous cultivars that will be useful in succulent displays, such as *Aesculus* 'Canyon Pink', *Salvia* 'Pozo Blue', and *Eriogonum* 'Shasta Sulphur'—all brightly flowered and showy. A novel and showy introduction is a new intergeneric hybrid palo verde called *Parkinsidium* 'Desert Museum' a cross between three species of *parkinsonia* and *cercidium* with bright yellow sprays of pea flowers on green stems. It is in full flower at only three feet in height, which gives it a very promising future for smaller gardens. Bart O'Brien, concedes that RSABG years ago developed two ornamental prickly pear selections, one an extra-bristly grizzly bear cactus (to be introduced as *Opuntia erinacea* var. *ursina* 'Mike Hammit'), and an unusual and yet-to-be-named red-orange flowered *O. vaseyi* collected years ago near Palm Springs.

The fifty-five-acre California Plant Communities section consists of several spacious beds, most of them two or three acres, each representing a Southern California plant biome. However, due to a lack of signage it is difficult to distinguish one zone from another and to positively identify many of the plants. O'Brien, says this will soon be remedied with a signage project. Still, a closer look introduces one to a living plant geography book. It is in the plant communities section that we find the garden's most dramatic landscape, the Joshua Tree Woodland (it really looks like a natural woodland), where grow the most impressive yucca and giant beargrass (*Nolina parryi* ssp. *wolfii*) plantings to be seen in a cultivated garden not in the desert. The flowering specimens must be as old as the garden. This area should be visited in April or May when the rare and seldom seen giant beargrass from the Kingston Mountains sends up an eight-to-twelve-foot-tall fountain of thousands of diminutive creamy flowers.

Yucca brevifolia, best known as the Joshua tree, is seldom seen on the "semitropical" side of the San Gabriel and San Bernardino Mountains because it is adapted to a narrow band between 3,500 and 5,000 feet in the Mohave Desert. At RSABG, however, you can see how this yucca has adapted to growing in the decomposed granite of an alluvial plain. Apparently it offsets from rhizomes and eventually forms dense thickets, making a very attractive backdrop to the masses of yellow-orange mimulus flowers, as well as the soft, billowy grays of the great basin sagebrush (*Artemisia tridentata*). The Joshua tree was given its name by Mormon trekkers as they passed through the desert on their way from California to settle in Utah. To the Mormons, the humanoid twisted branching suggested the prophet Joshua pointing the way to the Promised Land (Utah).

In April, the Joshua Tree Woodland comes alive with one of the lovely creamy-pink-flowered California lilacs, *Ceanothus megacarpus*. Many of the Joshua trees were moved from the Orange County location about fifty years ago. They thrive, probably assisted by summer heat, lack of water, and their excellent sunny and well-drained location. In early spring the stem tips produce soft white to greenish white flowers that some say are edible. I do find some kinds of yucca blossoms good to eat, and they can be a nice addition to a salad. Mojave Desert Indians harvested the melon-sized inflorescences and cooked them. Mescal pits throughout the Southwest attest to the fact that many Indian peoples harvested and roasted agave hearts; they were of a molasses-like consistency and guaranteed a food supply through the winter.

In the early 1870s a British paper mill was built to convert Joshua tree pulp to newsprint. Several issues of the London Telegraph were printed on paper made from Joshuas, but fortunately for the trees the project was too costly and was given up. World War I brought another attempt at Joshua tree exploitation when it was discovered that the wood made excellent bone splints. When soaked the fibrous wood could be molded to any shape, and when dried, it retained its original shape, for use by the U.S. Army to splint battlefield bone fractures.

RSABG does have a cactus garden, all natives of course, on the eastern side of the garden. Unfortunately, it is in desperate need of renovation and gets too much shade from surrounding trees and overgrown shrubs. It might be botanically correct, but compass barrels do not grow in shade. There are some interesting chollas for someone who might want to buck the cactophobia attitude, such as the cane cholla (*Opuntia versicolor*) and the coast cholla (*O. prolifera*), which grow well in nondesert areas. The teddy bear cholla (*O. bigelovii*), common to true desert landscaping, does not grow well in areas with frequent overcast skies and winter rains. Bart concedes that the cactus garden is too heavily shaded and in time will be phased out, the plants most likely being incorporated into the floristic provinces.

The garden has a bright future under the leadership of current director Clement Hamilton, formerly of the University of Washington Urban Horticulture Program. I hope that publicizing knowledge of native plants and California's succulents will figure in their cultivar introduction program. There are many possibilities.

A rare sight in a Mediterranean climate: vigorous clumps of Joshua tree (*Yucca brevifolia*).

Huntington Desert Garden, San Marino

The Huntington Desert Garden had an ambivalent beginning. It was one of several theme gardens at the Henry E. Huntington winter home and ranch in the genteel agrarian San Gabriel Valley, east of Los Angeles. Before long the uncertainty gave way to a series of renovations and expansions that continues today, making The Huntington Desert Garden one of the most fascinating landscapes and most significant botanical collections in the world. It was begun by William Hertrich, who was trained in Europe as a landscape gardener. He arrived at the San Marino Ranch in 1904, highly recommended as a ranch foreman to railroad and land baron Henry Huntington. The seven-hundred-acre Shorb, or San Marino, Ranch had been purchased by Huntington just the previous year. Hertrich excelled at ranch management and displayed cleverness in dealing with his powerful employer, who was not so much a garden savant as one who knew his mind and what he wanted to see on his ranch grounds. Hertrich could quickly determine what Huntington did and did not like. He knew Huntington loved the native oaks (the beaux arts mansion, now the main art gallery, had to be sited so a nearby oak would not be disturbed) but did not like cacti (years earlier he unforgettably backed into some heavily armored prickly pears while supervising a Southern Pacific Railway construction crew).

By 1905, Hertrich, in addition to his other duties on the ranch, had laid out new gardens and plantings that included lily ponds, a palm garden, and a rose garden. Hertrich had a consuming interest in cacti and one day suggested to Huntington that the barren slope above the duck pond reservoir be developed as a cactus garden. Huntington was negative, but Hertrich argued that nothing else would grow on the barren slope and that it was an eyesore from the ranch entrance. Huntington gave in and allowed a trial planting. In 1905, construction began on what was to become one of the largest, if not the largest, garden collection of specimen cacti and succulents anywhere in the world.

The initial planting consisted of three hundred cacti that scarcely covered the slope. Finding suitable specimens put Hertrich in competition with other collectors who had impressive collections and displays of native and exotic desert plants. During what might best be called the Age of Cactus Garden Wars (from about 1900 to 1930), wealthy estate owners, such as Bradbury,

Doheny, and Huntington vied to achieve bragging rights for owning and showing off the finest collection of cacti and succulents money could buy. Deserts suffered from the pilfering, and nurseries prospered from the wars of the entreprenurial titans in search of their Eden.

When Huntington discovered that visitors to the ranch began taking greater interest in his new collection of spiny plant specimens than his elegant and expensive paintings and books, he turned Hertrich loose on what was to become Huntington's newest collecting craze with the goal to build the best collection and garden in the world. Hertrich, with Huntington's patronage, was not limited to local suppliers and local deserts, the source of landscape material for most gardens at this time. His resources included Huntington's Pacific Electric Railway and the Southern Pacific: No collector should be without them. The railroads funneled his art and book collections from east to west. Having at Hertrich's disposal any form of transport required for moving plants and rock put him way ahead of the competitors. In 1908 he collected three carloads of native cacti to be planted on the hillside garden. Later he went to Mexico and returned with hundreds of plants, including the golden barrel cactus (*Echinocactus grusonii*)—a rare instance of its being collected in the wild. Today it is depleted in its natural habitat in central Mexico though, as perhaps the best-known cactus, hundreds of thousands are seed grown in the wholesale nursery trade. The plants Hertrich brought from Mexico could have been one of the sources of commercial seed.

Once Huntington had established the purpose of the garden, Hertrich set up growing facilities for acquisition of seeds and plants from the great European nurseries, e.g., Haage and Schmidt in Germany and Franz de Laet in Belgium. Many plants subsequently came from cactus nurseries in Mexico and botanic gardens in South Africa. But the winds of fashion change and time catches up with even the wealthiest garden makers. In a few years many of Huntington's competitors' collections were up for sale and Huntington could take his pick. In 1915, the U.S. Department of Agriculture began the practice of sending new introductions to the Huntington. Also about this time the garden's importance as a collection became known to botanists, and serious cactus collectors began donating and exchanging plants—a practice that

South American *Puya alpestris*; the robust inflorescence provides its own bird perches.

Previous page: The landscape effect of
ninety-five years of growth and care.

Succulents native to Mexico; note flowering *Agave chrysoglossa*; behind it on right is accession # 1, *A. ceslii* var. *albicans*.

continues to this day. By 1931, serious record keeping and plant labeling had begun, giving an estate collection the new status of botanic garden. The campaign to build the finest desert garden in the world was one of Huntington's greatest legacies. He outpaced and outlived his competitors and their interests.

In 1925, the duck pond was drained and landscaped with specimen cacti that had outgrown the original display. The new beds were slightly contoured, and smooth granite rocks continued to be used for the borders. The pond went from riparian habitat to desert and added another four acres to the garden. The resultant maze of little islands still survives intact, and the area is referred to by staff as the Lower Garden. Some magnificent specimens in the Lower Garden are still growing out their years, such as the braced massive dragon's blood tree (*Dracaena draco*), several gigantic tree yuccas (*Yucca filifera*) originally planted around the pond-reservoir in 1912. One yucca is nearly sixty feet tall, making it among the world's tallest succulents. An ancient night blooming cereus (*Cereus xanthocarpus*), one of the largest in cultivation and the largest and probably oldest cactus in the Desert Garden, struggles to survive; it dates from the 1880s or earlier.

Some of the original garden layout survives in the southeast corner of the estate, consisting of stepped paths lined with smooth granite boulders plucked from nearby arroyos. The planting scheme, as exemplified in early archive photos, shows a rather stiff arrangement, sacrificing size to orderly plantings with individual specimens planted equidistantly, in tidy rows. Such a stiff arrangement could not last; for example, the more vigorous agaves and yuccas smothered the slow-growing barrel cacti and no doubt provided incentive to further expand the garden. This adherence to formalism did not end upon Huntington's death in 1927; it managed to survive, though in more muted manifestations, until the 1960s.

Today the nearly twelve-acre Desert Garden, and its three thousand species, is a museum of living architecture and a living botanical reference library. It is also part of the Desert Plant Collection, which includes a public conservatory, research and conservation collections, and a special project called International Succulent Introductions. Furthermore, there are propagation and research collections not on public display, adding perhaps another two thousand species, which adds up to a botanical ark holding one of the most important collections of succulents in world. The gardens and conservatory collection leaves the unprepared visitor dazed in amazement that there exist in the plant world so many forms, colors, and camouflage patterns, all of which are nothing more than survival strategies in a parched environment.

The Desert Garden collections are carefully labeled and documented. Since the 1930s it has been a Huntington policy to seek out plant acquisitions that had locality data, i.e., species collected in a recorded locality. In 1931, Eric Walther, botanist at San Francisco's Golden Gate Park and the California Academy of Sciences, set up an accession catalogue and data system still in use today. It is now supplemented by computer-based record-keeping and mapping systems with plant and seed accessions surpassing 85,000 and forming a critical resource for *ex situ* conservation.

The special Huntington project called International Succulent Introductions (ISI) distributes yearly a catalogue of rare and new species and hybrids, often introduced to collectors for the first time. Many introductions are garden worthy. John Trager, collections curator and manager of ISI each year acquires and propagates fifty or sixty new or rare species and hybrids. He is careful that all seed and seedlings imported by the Huntington are collected with the proper permits, have valuable locality documentation, and are properly inspected by U.S. authorities. With the establishment of ISI at the Huntington, plant distribution to specialist collectors is facilitated through publication of its plant availability lists on the Internet, with many new introductions now sent throughout the world.

The numerous garden projects and routines for maintaining the plants' health begin with daily cleanup, such as plucking sycamore leaves from cactus plantings using veterinarian's forceps. Much of the area is painstakingly weeded by hand. The many collages of groundcover succulents, including ice plants, echeverias, sedums, and graptopetalums, require constant grooming and replanting. Water is a continuing worry. People ask, "Why do cacti need so much water when they hardly get any in the desert?" The answer is that most of the cacti and succulents growing in the garden do not fit the desert stereotype. Many deserts and drylands experience seasonal monsoons and high humidity; they require far more moisture than found in the desert Southwest. Besides, succulents look perkier and grow better here when given supplemental waterings and feedings throughout the year.

Eighty-year-old Golden Barrel cacti;
top left *Agave bractosa*.

According to Joe Clements, curator of the Desert Garden, the public garden—less than half the garden—is watered at least one hour weekly, while the off-limits areas are watered for twelve hours once a month. In addition, gardeners often spend part of an afternoon hand watering stonecrops and other sensitive succulents to keep them plump and looking their best.

Since it was first planted over ninety years ago, the Huntington Desert Garden has undergone a number of expansion phases, accompanied by evolving concepts of design, changes in taste, plant availability, and cumulative shifts in appearance provided by the gardener's spade and hoe. Survival of the fittest gives the garden's older specimens much of their character and plays an important role in the makeup of the displays. In the first half of the twentieth century, the garden suffered the ill effects of devastating freezes, most notably the 1949 freeze where the garden was under snow and over two-thirds of it was destroyed or damaged. During World War II, maintenance suffered from the loss of staff, and the garden did not begin to recover until Myron Kimnach, now editor of the *Journal of the Cactus and Succulent Society of America*, became director of the gardens in 1962. He dramatically upgraded standards of gardening, landscaping, and curation for all the gardens.

Dr. James Folsom, current director of the botanic gardens, is developing a new research and administrative center for all the gardens, and also is making major innovations such as redesigning the old Desert Garden paths to make them more user friendly. He is experimenting with different materials, colors, and textures for the paths, and already this has produced impressive results. In the near future a huge chunk of the lower garden for the first time will be opened to the public. Joe Clements says this project will require substantial relandscaping to make it more appealing. The area to be opened contains many of the rare and exotic puyas collected by T. Harper Goodspeed, noted California botanist and author of the popular *Plant Hunters in the Andes*. He noted their landscape potential for California gardens on his expeditions to Chile and Peru, and the Huntington has a premier selection of his recommendations. Regrettably, they have grown at the Huntington for over sixty years and are yet to be popular in gardens, in spite of their pulse-stopping metallic blue, green, and violet flowers. Also located in the soon-to-be-opened area, is a remnant of the original garden Hertrich laid out in 1905, which Jim Folsom plans to preserve and display as an artifact of late Victorian desert gardening in Southern California.

In 1929, four years after the duck pond was drained and planted, the maze of beds was diminished by construction of a broader central walk, resulting in the closing of some of the paths. For most of its one-third-mile length each side was bermed. Hertrich personally placed perhaps a thousand tons of volcanic rock thought to have come from the Arizona desert. There are no records that clearly show the origin of the rock; we only know it has never been duplicated. Hertrich apparently got the Pacific Electric railway company to contruct a spur line into the Lower Garden in order to bring the rock-filled freight cars directly into the garden! The rock and, at times, cacti came first class directly to the job site.

A year later, Hertrich completed of one of the largest (certainly the longest) rockeries in the country and planted it solid with cacti, making it known from that day on as the pièce de résistance of cactus displays (especially golden barrel and pincushion cacti). Prior to 1930, there were few terraced or raised rockeries constructed especially for cacti—the concept was reserved for alpines and tufted herbaceous perennials in the east and in temperate Europe. Today, the raised rockery is regarded as the best design concept for growing and displaying cacti.

The Huntington Desert Garden is now divided into sixty-two beds, or sections, some planted as thematic displays, such as South American cacti and bromeliads, cacti from Mexico, aloes and other succulents found only in Africa, succulents from Baja California and California, and succulents from Madagascar and the Canary Islands. There is also a section devoted to testing and displaying succulent groundcovers. Behind the scenes are historic collections of the genra *Agave*, *Nolina*, *Dasylirion*, and *Yucca*—all very old specimens that could be grown only in a large botanic garden or arboretum. Beyond these thematic displays, the primary design focus of the garden is a celebration of the beauty of succulent plants from the terrifying twelve-inch spines of *Ferocactus rectispinus* to the soft and voluptuous *Graptopetalum fittkaui*.

The Desert Garden is dominated by agaves, aloes, boojum trees, hardy euphorbias, forests of tree cerei, bristly thickets of golden barrels, mesembs, stonecrops, terrestrial bromeliads that spread like glaciers, and gigantic tree yuccas. It sounds like a veritable cornucopia of nonsensical names from some dream adventure. However, this is no dream. The agaves represent over ninety years of acquiring specimens from nurseries, gardens, and from the wild. The Huntington's collection is one of the largest in the world and contains many ancient plantings of unknown origin and identity. The diversity of the agave collection results from years of research by Howard Scott Gentry, author of the definitive monograph, *Agaves of Continental North America* (1982). The most spectacular agaves are the giant pulque agaves, *Agave mapisaga* var. *lisa* and *A. tecta*. They are the giants of the

Winter color in the Desert Garden. The tree
yuccas (*Yucca filifera*) were planted in 1912.

genus, so large that they are relegated to the background, otherwise they would overwhelm an entire bed. The flower stalk is a veritable tree, branched and rising to eighteen feet. Collectively, the flowers produce gallons of nectar, a soft drink station for birds (especially hummingbirds), bats, insects, and small rodents. Such an inflorescence is a tree of life in the xeric ecosystem; without the sugary nectar as one of the few sources of moisture in that environment, survival for some birds and other animal species would not be possible.

The Aztecs of pre-Hispanic Mexico venerated the goddess of pulque, who is depicted in the Aztec codices emerging, like the flower stalk, from the center of a large agave. Pulque is a naturally fermented beerlike beverage still popular in Mexico and consumed since prehistoric times. A double-distilled product it is made from the crushed hearts of *Agave tequilana* that are called *piñas*. The identity of the product, clearly com-memorated in the species name, is native to Jalisco, Mexico, and is a relatively recent additon to Mexico's ancient agave economy. Its distillate was first introduced to the United States in the 1870s as mescal wine, but it was renamed mescal brandy and was formally debuted at the 1892 Columbian Exposition. Its name was changed again, and we *norteamericanos* are the principal consumers of this drink: tequila.

Agave parryi var. truncata is a landscape treasure that originated in the Huntington. This is perhaps the most beautiful century plant ever brought into cultivation and, after many years of being overlooked, is now grown in commercial nurseries. Years ago, agave expert Howard Scott Gentry collected it in the state of Durango in Mexico and gave it to the Huntington as an unnamed species. Finally it flowered, and he was then able to describe it as a new kind of century plant. It has an attribute shared by no other cultivated agave: it is the only known plant—it has never been rediscovered—and may have been the only example in the wild. Today it survives solely in gardens.

Many parts of the Desert Garden hold important collections, most of which are integrated into the thematic displays. While these collections are not taxonomically arranged, the visitor at every turn sees unexpected as well as rarely seen specimens, such as *Neobuxbaumia scoparia*—possibly the only plant of this slow-growing columnar cactus in cultivation and one that Hertrich

may have brought from Mexico before 1920. A few paces away, *Dracaena serrulata*, an extremely rare dragon's blood tree from Yemen, in ancient times utilized for its astringent red resin. Many other species in the Desert Garden are extremely rare in cultivation, such as *cleistocactus* and *borzicactus* from Peru, Argentina, and Bolivia. For some reason, these cacti are not popular with collectors—perhaps because they are best suited for a landscaped garden, not a greenhouse assemblage of potted plants. Their scarcity is all the more reason to grow them at the Huntington and other botanic gardens. The seed was originally collected in the wild, making these cacti priceless for conservation purposes.

The African succulent displays and the Madagascar collection are found in the upper garden, the last part of the Desert Garden to be developed by Hertrich (but not open to the public until 1966). This part of the garden features one of the most dramatic displays of winter flowering aloes to be seen anywhere in the world. The upper garden is also the location of the conservatory. There are plantings of shrubby euphorbias (beware of the milky sap) and the endangered and endemic Madagascar pachypodiums and didierias, spiny ocotillo-like plants. Only the native lemurs, which climb them, seem to not mind the fortress like armature of long thorns.

At the top of the central walk and near the garden entrance are some magnificent succulent grapes (*Cyphostemma juttae*), but do not look for vines. These are called pachycaul, or caudiciform, succulents, and their enormous thick, floppy leaves are deciduous, leaving a huge rocklike caudex. They eventually grow to vast proportions and some specimens from a distance can pass for posing bodybuilders. In September and October a crop of bright-red grapelike fruits appear and look good enough to eat. Do not, unless you want a burned mouth.

Aloes form the backbone of winter color in the garden. They consist of over four hundred species and hybrids, and are planted as colorful accents throughout the garden. The shrubby and arborescent forms are often used as background and buffer plants, and the effect is one of the cheeriest winter flower displays to be seen anywhere in the country. During this period at least two hundred aloe species and hundreds of plants are in flower. People often ask when is the best time to see the Desert Garden

Puya berteroniana in flower.

and I say at two periods—December to January, and again April to June, when cacti, puyas, yuccas, and agaves are flowering.

The garden's most impressive aloe is the quiver tree (*Aloe dichotoma*), a small dichotomously branched tree with a massively thick trunk growing near the Palm Garden. It is native to Namaqualand and parts of the Namib Desert. It flowers in the fall, earlier than most aloes, when its eerie thick, stubby branches are ablaze with brilliant canary yellow blossoms. It is one of the treasures in the collection and was planted in the early 1930s. Today it may be is the largest specimen outside southern Africa. The largest aloes of all are planted as a stately grove as one first enters the Desert Garden from the entry pavilion. The great tree aloe (*A. bainesii*) is possibly the largest of all succulents. Its rough eucalyptus-like bark contrasts with the readily recognizable rosettes of aloe leaves and pinkish blossoms. One field botanist said she had seen plants growing in jungly ravines in the northern Transvaal that were ninety-five feet tall.

Occasionally the tall single-rosette aloes, such a *A. ferox* and *A. marlothii*, become top heavy and collapse. If the crown of thick heavy leaves has not been destroyed, it is cut away and replanted. By the following year the crown will be growing again. Many of the single-stemmed aloes with candelabra flowers in the upper garden would be forty or fifty feet tall if they could hold themselves up. This garden practice of replanting the crown keeps the single stemmed aloes alive and flowering for decades beyond their normal life span.

My favorite plant in the African section is easily overlooked. In fact, for years no one, including the gardeners, knew it existed until the director spied an unusual vine growing in a tree. When the tree was cleared, it revealed a long-lost elephant's foot (*Dioscorea*, formerly *Testudinaria, elephantipes*) that turned out to be the largest example outside its native South Africa. It has an enormous tree-trunk-like caudex, covered with thick woody reticulations, making it look like something between an elephant and the Hunchback of Notre Dame. Each year several short vines grow from the apex, dying back in late spring. How it ever survived freezes, flooding rains, snow, and neglect for nearly seventy years in a poorly drained spot is a mystery. The elephant's foot is difficult to grow and is customarily relegated to pot culture. It belongs to the yam family, and the pulp is eaten by Africans. This is one plant that will never be moved; any

Rare *Mammillaria backebergii* flowering in the pincushion rockery.

Dracaena draco, one of the oldest and largest plants in the Desert Garden. Acquired 1912.

Flowering *Wigginsia sellowii* (*Parodia erinacea*). Wigginsias reseed themselves in the garden.

landscaping will have to work around it. One can only marvel that such a form exists at all. The plant is a "he," and needs a female plant that will provide fruit and seed. So far we have only come up with males. The desert can be a lonely place indeed.

Even if the African section experiences fall in our spring, sufficient flower activity remains to present nice color in May and June. *Aloe* 'Rooikappie' ('Red Head'), a low prolific aloe hybrid from a Transvaal nursery, flowers year-round and is highly recommended for local landscaping. The leafy 'crown of thorns' euphorbias, prickly succulent shrubs endemic to Madagascar, also are sources of spring and early summer color. There are several species, some quite rare, with flowers (actually petalloid *cyathophylls*) varying from bright, cheery red to pink, yellow, and white. The showiest are *Euphorbia milii* var. *hislopii*, and *E. milii* 'Apache Red,' a cultivar developed by E.C. Hummel, one of Southern California's most successful succulent growers and hybridizers. Another spring flowering euphorbia is *E. lambii*, which has naturalized in the Huntington and is now popular in California gardens. It is from the Canary Islands, and plants resemble open umbrellas with a dichotomous branching habit suggesting the giant dragon tree. Its cyathia flowers are lime green and add an exotic, softening element to the landscape. A late spring flowering aloe is *A. camperi*, native to east Africa, particularly the Ethiopian highlands, and has long-stemmed masses of pale orange blossoms. *A. camperi* is slow growing and in time forms a small thicket of offsets.

In the uphill portion of the garden are a couple of pre-rancho sycamore trees whose messiness is tolerated for they, along with a few native coast live oaks, provide winter and summer shelter for more delicate succulents, such as crassulas, sedums, echeverias, senecios, as well as tender Brazilian cacti. Here there is mid to late summer color provided by the showy bright red flowering, flat-topped head of the airplane-propeller plant (*Crassula falcata*).

Midway down the central walk, on the right, begins part of the Mexican cactus display, and on the left, the South American cacti. Many South American cacti have ribbed stems and are densely spiny and shrubby. Their flowers are mostly tubular or funnelform, the most colorful displays being *cleistocactus*, *borzicactus*, and *echinopsis*. The globular white- and pink-flowering species are known as Easter lily cacti and were introduced in the nineteenth century.

The newest additions to the garden are the shockingly colorful *echinopsis* cultivars called Schick hybrids. When fully established they will be one of the most colorful cactus displays ever planted. The hybrids were developed and meticulously documented over the past twenty years by Robert Schick, who began to make hybrid cactus crosses to create sensational floral color. The Schick *echinopsis* hybrids are introduced yearly through the Huntington's International Succulent Introductions and are popular at the Annual Plant Sale. The intensely glowing, oranges, reds, and yellow hybrid *echinopsis* flower in spring through early summer; the blossom event is unparalleled in the history of the garden.

In spring visitors should be certain to observe in the lower garden the terrestrial bromeliad displays. These are puyas, pitcairneas, and dyckias, all putting on a unique Huntington flower show, for nowhere will you see agave-like bromeliads with flowers and flower spikes of such incredible hues. If you are an expert photographer, you might faithfully capture in April or May the chartreuse and blue-green flowers of puya with their unique metallic sheen. The showiest species do not have flowers around the branch tips; these naked branch ends have become bird perches to facilitate more effective pollen gathering.

Garden Director Jim Folsom is committed to conserving the rare plants in the garden; in 1995, he initiated a desert garden survey, its purpose being to locate, confirm names, and label every plant. He is also initiating a program of path realignment and design, eliminating dangerous steps and extending them to parts of the garden never before open to the public, such as the southeast section of the garden. Part of this area includes a surviving portion of the original garden, which he intends to restore to its original 1905 design. In the future, a new conservatory will be built. The Desert Garden is a complex of traditions and disciplines, requiring visionary leadership and dedicated hardworking plant enthusiasts. It played, and still does, an important role in garden design, plant selection and introduction, botanical research and illustration. In the new millenium its possibilities will increase as interest turns to using drought-tolerant plants in general landscaping, placing greater emphasis on *ex situ* conseravtion, and emphasizing education in economic and medicinal plants as well as plant biodiversity.

Scene in the Lower Desert Garden that once was Huntington's duck pond.

San Gabriel Mission, San Gabriel

The San Gabriel Mission is one of the earliest of twenty-one Franciscan missions built in California between the Mexico border and just north of San Franciso Bay. Each mission was about a day's horseback ride from another, one of its purposes being to provide rest, lodging, and food for the weary traveler. San Gabriel Mission, constructed in 1771, has barely survived total destruction from numerous earthquakes, and now, at long last, is nearing full restoration.

Father Junipero Serra, and others who followed, introduced many plants to California for food, fiber, and medicines. A number of them originated in the Mediterranean region, especially Spain and Portugal. Others came from the West Indies and Mexico. There is little doubt the missionaries introduced the spineless Indian fig cactus (*Opuntia ficus indica*), also called the mission cactus, and most likely its spiny form *O. megacantha*; the century plant (*Agave americana*); and the medicinal aloe (*Aloe vera*). Because of their relative hardiness the opuntias most likely originated in Mexico; the aloe originated in the Mediterranean region, where it had been brought by Phoenician traders.

The opuntias, their pads or flattened stems called nopales and the fruits called tunas were (and still are) used as food and fodder and also for security fencing around the missions. Cactus hedges were effective in keeping marauders out of and livestock in the mission compound. In fact, in 1809, several hundred acres of mission land were planted with protective mission cactus hedges up to twelve feet tall, to keep out wild horses. The Cape Aloe (*Aloe arborescens*) was probably brought to the missions by Anglo-American or European travelers; it had been introduced to Europe from South Africa.

Historically the missions were associated with the Spanish Empire, and the establishment of missions throughout the Southwest was a means of creating a Spanish presence and of maintaining a constituency (the converted Indians) to thwart U.S. or Russian designs on western North America at the end of the eighteenth century. At the San Gabriel Mission, I could not resist asking mission curator Helen Nelson if the cactus gardens, common features at most missions, had any connection to monastic duty or meditation. She responded that all mission gardens are recent developments contrived to attract tourists in spite of being planted by the mission fathers. Most are quite charming, but the San Gabriel Mission's cactus garden reflects a true love of succulents.

Missions were designed as part fortress and part factory, where the most products required for survival were manufactured, raised, or grown. There were no pleasure gardens, such as the tourist sees today in most of the restored missions. The outdoor spaces, according to Helen Nelson, were strictly utilitarian. However, there were vegetable and medicinal plant gardens; fruit trees, including citrus; and flower beds for altar decorations. In addition, there were agaves grown for fiber. Every mission had its palm trees, for their leafy fronds were needed each year for the celebration of Palm Sunday.

Throughout the mission grounds are plantings of cacti and succulents, but one large courtyard—once a work area for such activities as tanning leather, making candles, and cooking—is divided into several rectangular semiformal flat beds, each densely planted with an interesting cross section of cacti common to cultivation. The cactus gardens were begun over forty years ago by Father Montoya and were completed in the 1980s by Father Raymond Catalan, occasionally assisted by the Huntington's Joe Clements.

The garden is interesting for its specimen tree euphorbias, such as *Euphorbia tetragona*, with its thin, lanky four-angled branches jutting from a thick central trunk; a pencil tree (*E. tirucalli*) growing against a sunny chapel wall; and shrubby cow's horn euphorbia (*E. grandicornis*). Also of interest are flowering and fruiting specimens of the spiny fat-trunked Madagascar palm (*Pachypodium lameri*). Landscaping with euphorbias and pachypodiums can be a bit tricky; one should be careful to keep them away from paths so unwary children and adults cannot come in contact with the stems, flowers, or fruit. They can be dangerous.

Cow's Tongue (*Opuntia lindheimeri* var. *linguiformis*) from Texas.

Two kinds of blue kleinia (*Senecio mandraliscae* and *S. vitalis*) lend softness but are kept from spreading as dense groundcovers. The usual prickly pear cacti are there, including the cow's tongue (*Opuntia lindheimeri var. linguiformis*), which forms a great mass near the crumbling and unrestored candle and soap furnaces. Also present are hyperpruned mission cacti and other opuntias known for their edible fruits. The white-variegated century plant (*Agave americana* var. *medio picta* 'Alba') adds a cheerful element. A flowering size *Puya alpestris* and the orange-flowered peruvian ceroid (*Corryocactus ayacuchoensis*) are hints of Huntington influence. After all, the Huntington is only a few minutes drive from the mission.

Helen Nelson is giving serious thought to removing the cactus gardens and returning the space, for education purposes, to its original concept as a processing and manufacturing area. True, there are problems in the cactus garden's layout, suggested by overzealous pruning and overplanting with succulents that require more space than allowed. Removing the more recent gardens is controversial as there are two schools of thought in mission restoration: restore to original function as a work facility or retain gardens to beautify grounds but give them a warmer more attractive look. Mission restoration, which had included the planting of gardens, has been underway since the last century. Perhaps gardens that were part of earlier restoration efforts should be considered in the context of a mission tradition that contributed greatly to Southern California's architectural heritage—and likewise to California's landscape heritage.

Views at the Mission: right foreground note
effective use of herbacious perennials for color.

Being an old hand at the Huntington and quite at home in gardens and buildings connected to California's and America's heritage, I must admit the Getty Center and its modernist gardens were a bit of a shock. Unlike the Huntington, the Getty Center is plunked down on a 110-acre Brentwood hilltop and has a commanding view of the perpetually congested 405 freeway. From the point of view of futuristic thinking, design, and American know-how, it is a most impressive statement. Yet, I fear what the statement really means. There is little in the design that connects it to historic California; the connection is more to Hollywood sci-fi fantasy as a potential rest stop for passing aliens from outer space.

The Getty is one of the most prestigious and important art museums in the world. Designed by noted architect Richard Meier, it was completed in 1997 at a cost of one billion dollars. It consists of the museum, the Getty Research Institute for the History of Art and the Humanities, the Getty Conservation Institute, the Getty Education Institute for the Arts, the Getty Information Institute, and the Getty Grant Program. In short, its impact on the art world is enormous. It is open to the public by reservation and is accessible only by a specially designed tram.

The Getty Center's most conspicuous feature is its use of a bright, beige-colored Italian limestone called travertine. Sixteen-thousand tons of it cover 1.2 million square feet of wall and paving space throughout the facility. Its only naturalistic attribute is the occasional presence of fossilized seashells, fish, and even leaves.

The formal cactus gardens are planted in three descending terraces, two of them connected by a broad staircase of brightly polished travertine hugging a wall of the same material and leading to an overlook that provides a view of the more distant cactus garden. Approaching the overlook is not the sort of experience one expects; it is either suicidal or homicidal depending upon the powerful wind tunnel effect rising unpredictably from the canyons below. Besides feeling an instinctive urge to grab hold of something to keep from being flung to the prickly depths below, I was overwhelmed by a sense of existential desolation, produced by the post-nuclear-holocaust architecture and the formal plantation landscape reminiscent of wholesale cactus nurseries.

The gardens are not without interest, however. They were designed by Laurie Olin, working under Emmet Wemple, and

Preparing for war—the lower cactus terrace.

presumably the design concept is purely artistic, the cacti substituting for colored cement. On the lower level, masses of golden barrel cacti are set out like a commercial growing ground, appearing to hold off an attack of variegated century plants, with pincer-like sweep of hallucinogenic San Pedro cactus (*Trichocereus pachanoi*) pushing from one side and oozing masses of prickly pear from the other cutting off all hope of escape. I feel sorry for the gardeners who must maintain these unnatural associations. There is comic relief in knowing that the agaves will flower and die and that such a mass flowering will probably cause even more congestion on the 405 by gawking comuters.

On the two upper terraces we find a grove of tree aloe (*Aloe bainesii*) and tree euphorbia (*Euphorbia ingens*). The tree aloe is interesting simply because it appears to be a dwarf form, possibly a new variety, of this species. Beneath is a powdery blue groundcover of blue kleinia (*Senecio mandraliscae*) and a quirky chalk-like lavender-gray, stone mulch. Eventually something has to give with these tree succulents; before long they will form an inpenetrable knot of vegetation, threatening the prevalent control and manipulation of nature theme.

Artist Robert Irwin of Escondido designed the Central Garden, which is separate from the cactus garden terraces. It is unclear whether it is proper to call it a garden or a work of art using plants as paints to color and texture. To have a great variety of plants in such close association requires three full-time gardeners in order to preserve the effect. It reminds me of Rose Parade floats. The most attractive part of this garden, bisected by a naturalistic creek or ravine, is well planted with a great variety of herbaceous perennials and soft-leaf succulents pleasant to the eye. The quality of the plant selection and their immaculate care are reminiscent of the conservatory plantings at the Las Vegas Bellagio casino.

What I find remarkable about this section of the Central Garden is the extensive use of soft-leaf succulents among an incredible array of colorful and unusual cultivars of so many different herbaceous perennials. Incredibly, the muted pastel colors and rosette shapes of the succulents work well with the herbaceous plants but otherwise have no logical connection to them. Ruby red cannas and pink starburst displays of Canary Island geranium add pleasure to the noisy cascade and its uplifting rhythms. Throughout are planted soft mounds of miniature statice: hebe and kangaroo paw (*Anigozanthos*) yield exotic violets and royal purples. There are perfectly grown mounds of variegated grasses and the blackest black mondo grass I have ever seen. Intermixed are chalky white rosettes of the Baja California native siempreviva (*Dudlyea brittonii*). There are clumps of the once popular but now nearly disappeared *Echeveria* 'Perle von Nurnburg', creeping Asiatic sedums, aeoniums, pachyverias, and echeverias. At the very bottom of the cascade is an incendiary specimen of Euphorbia 'Sticks on Fire'. The result is beautiful, dramatic, and high maintenance herbaceous perennial stream bank that with the water feature cascades nearly one hundred yards from the top to where it empties into the Azalea Pool below.

A path constructed of a patchwork of green slate paving stones and edged with upright strips of Cor-Ten industrial steel zigzags in and out of the cascade, from one side to the other. At each crossing, the rapidly descending stream makes a different complex of sounds. At the very bottom are two flat paving stones on which Robert Erwin etched the motto: "Ever present never twice the same; Ever changing never less than whole." It is unclear whether this statement is about the level of spiritual awareness one obtains zigzagging in and out of the garden or is a job order that is part of the gardener's daily routine. Also, the message of the garden raises profound questions about the future of public space and public landscape; it raised in my mind the totalitarian control of nature through privatization. In short, there was so much control in the design that *I* felt controlled.

Overleaf: Use of *Dudleya brittonii*, *echeveria*, *graptoveria*, *Kalanchoe pumila*, *sedum*, and *sempervivum* to create a collage effect.

Getty Center Cactus Garden, Los Angeles 103

Modelo Shales, Pacific Palisades

This lovely two-acre succulent garden in Pacific Palisades overlooking the Pacific Ocean is built on the scene of a natural disaster, a landslide that occurred in 1962. The garden was the idea of then-owners Boyd and Mary Ev Walker, who decided that succulents would help stabilize a slipping hillside below their residence slope. The slope was rebuilt and the succulent garden begun. Gardening and landscaping with succulents soon became a labor of love and a shared passion. The idea of using succulents came easy to the Walkers, as Boyd was a marine biologist at UCLA, an expert on the Sea of Cortez, which separates Baja California from mainland Mexico. It is impossible to spend time in Baja without becoming fascinated by the strange thorny shapes of giant cardons, boojums, elephant trees, and visnagas marching to the desert shore and commandeering the desert islands.

The Walker garden, now called Modelo Shales, perhaps to commemorate (or placate) the slippery interface that caused more than one landslide on the property, evolved over many years into a very attractive succulent border around the lawn. The extensive use of rock, brought from all over Southern California by the Walkers, transformed the precarious terrain into a spectacular garden of pleasing combinations of soft succulents interplanted with spiky agaves, yuccas, and furcraeas. There are few true cacti here, except for a cereus and golden barrel or two; their diminished presence highlights an unusual thematic softness of pastel color and smooth leaves. Individual plantings are situated in small masses with no bare earth showing between the numerous kinds represented. I am reminded of the groundcover display bed at the Huntington and can see that the same softness theme is successfully employed in a home garden.

The garden enjoys the ocean breezes, and the plant selection represents species best suited for coastal areas. The Canary Island dragon tree is suitable for close proximity to the ocean, and several robust umbrella-shaped specimens define the garden and give elegance to the entrance. Other large specimens include tree nolina (*Nolina beldingii*), fortress-trunked tree aloes, the fan aloe (*Aloe plicatilis*), and a remarkable flowering specimen of the giant tree yucca (*Yucca filifera*). I found this last specimen most interesting because it is smaller than the monsters at the

A garden of soft succulents; note flesh-toned flower stalks of *Kalanchoe fedtschenkoi*.

The gentle effect of a garden planted exclusively with succulents—except for the non-succulent *Festuca cineria* (*F. glauca*).

Huntington that were acquired in 1912. Obviously, they did not come from the same area in Mexico. The snowy white pendent inflorescence is shorter, thus making this clone, a dwarf form, a good choice for the home garden.

Occasionally, Joe Clements, curator of the Huntington Desert Garden, visited and suggested changes; otherwise, it was the work of the Walkers. They were the real designers and the head gardeners and were responsible for a garden that is a way of life, not a designed landscape. A succulent garden without cacti is more caretaker friendly than a true cactus garden, where meditations are often interrupted by sharp painful jabs. The few spinescent succulents in the garden are not of the threatening kind. Such an example is the *Agave* 'Leopoldii II', one of the most charming agaves, which forms tight clusters of small rosettes with narrow leaves and numerous curled white threads.

Most of the succulents are kept in scale by being treated as bedding plants, a practice similar to that at the Huntington. Before they can become leggy or too tall, plants like *aeonium* are dug, their stems cut, allowed to callus, then replanted. The

Foreground: *Euphorbia milii* var. *hislopii*; middle left: *Furcraea selloa marginata*; middle right: *E lambii* and *Kalanchoe beharensis*.

Unidentified coral tree (*Erythrina*) gives structure
and bright color to a succulent garden.

arrangements of *aeonium*, *echeveria*, *graptoveria*, *pachyveria*, and *sedum* make for a cheery, inviting display that creates a Southern California succulent herbaceous border. This look is perpetuated through continuous reworking of the plantings.

To keep a lush look, the garden is watered for fifteen minutes or so two to four times a week. This procedure is workable when there are no cacti or caudiciforms. Stonecrops, softer-leaved agaves, and aloes handle extra water better than cacti. Bright sun and higher coastal humidity helps with the leaf color; some aloes, such as the wine-red-leaved *Aloe elgonica* and the bronze *A. cameronii*, are more robust and colorful nearer the ocean than farther inland. The soft succulents respond well to occasional fertilizing.

There is much more to the garden than a border. Narrow paths crisscross the steep slope making the garden easy for strolling and for inspecting the 150 aloe species that provide structure and welcome winter color. A slow walk through the garden reveals that every bit of earth is lovingly planted with some kind of succulent; for example, a well-concealed patch of grassy *Haworthia gracilis* (diminutive succulents related to aloe) carpets the exposed roots of a coral tree. Downy pinkish violet rosettes of delicate Jack Catlin aeonium hybrids make enviable displays. Good color and structure are provided by numerous robust red-flowered specimens of *Euphorbia milii* var. *hislopii*, and *E. milii* 'Apache Red'. Dramatic accent is provided by shrubby specimens of *Aeonium arboreum* 'Zwartkop', better known as the black aeonium, which along the coast achieves its darkest hues in full sun. In some parts of the garden, simple stepped retaining walls consist of broken chunks of sidewalk with bits of succulents tucked here and there in the cracks. Cork oaks planted near the house support cascading clumps of Spanish moss to enhance the garden's relaxed effect.

Modelo Shales illustrates how intensive daily maintenance shapes the richness of the displays and their success in a large space. The look and maintenance program give it something in common with the English herbaceous border. There is also the issue of what becomes of such a garden when the owners leave. Usually, succulent gardens last no longer than their owners, which causes the loss of irreplaceable plant material, including species collected in natural areas that have been swallowed by urban sprawl and plants fading from cultivation. Such gardens play a crucial role in *ex situ* conservation; that is, by caring for their plants their owners keep them alive for future generations. Fortunately, Modelo Shales is assured continuity because the new owner, Abby Sher, is dedicated to conserving it and to maintaining it to the Walker's standards.

Four scenes depicting various applications of succulents. Upper left: *Aloe bainesii* trunks form backdrop to succulent border; lower left: *erythrina* and *A. plicatilis* as dramatic accents; upper right: smaller succulents used as bedding plants; lower right: use of potted examples of more interesting specimens to adorn exterior of house.

Serra Gardens, Malibu

Our intention is to discuss public and private succulent gardens; but when a garden turns up that does not fit these categories but stretches the concepts of design and garden, it is worthy of discussion. Serra Gardens, a wholesale nursery just a mile inland from Pacific Coast Highway in Malibu, is one of these exceptions. The ten-acre nursery is built around a modest (for Malibu) residence and fills most of this hot, steep-walled secluded valley prone to brushfires. Notwithstanding the fires, Serra is a natural paradise for succulents. Its owner, Don Newcomber, is no ordinary grower; in fact, he is one of the few who specialize in succulents for landscaping, meaning that much of his stock of agaves, aloes, cacti, and other succulents are grown to maturity in the ground or in large containers. For those who desire and can afford a garden planted with mature specimens, Serra Gardens would provide some of the best choices.

Among the plants best suited to the mild-climate garden include numerous aloe species and hybrids, agaves—many now grown from seed and in need of cultivar names—colorful clumping terrestrial bromeliads like *dyckia* and *hechtia*, milk barrel and tree euphorbias, Canary Island euphorbias, groundcover mesembs, and shrubby genera in the stonecrop family that include *aeonium*, *crassula*, *echeveria*, *kalanchoe*, *pachyveria*, and *sedum*. However, the plant list at Serra Gardens is not limited to stock items one can find at the local garden center; there are offerings of rareties, like the Peruvian *Borzicactus tessellatus*, and the magnificent, large white-leaved *Agave guiengola* in two-foot boxes; then there are newly discovered species, such as *Aloe scabrifolia*, a result of Don's frequent contact with specialist collectors in his quest for the unusual.

Don Newcomber's laid-back nursery is reminiscent of Southern California nurseries of an earlier era. If it were not for his conducting sales over the Internet, he could pass for Ernest Braunton at Lyon and Cobbe's Hollywood growing ground in the early 1900s. The grounds are not intentionally landscaped; the "gardens" are scenes created from accidental combinations of unsold stock mixed with new plantings for the trade. Don often,

maybe too often, gets attached to some magnificent specimen, such as the giant East African cucurbit *Gerardanthus macrorhizus*, and it stays put in the nursery. Looking like a huge, smooth boulder it gives the place character.

The cumulative effect of years of unsold stock and ongoing replanting and interplanting of new stock gives the visitor the impression that this is not a nursery—that it doubles as a garden. One can stroll through the place in the late afternoon and experience amber-lit garden scenes typical to the small Malibu valley. There are palm trees and a grove of avocado trees lining a dirt lane; its deep shade is useful for Don's more delicate plants. There are specimen cacti, such as arborescent *borzicactus* and *cleistocactus*, some from specialty collections he has acquired that rival specimens in the Huntington. Don's milk barrel euphorbias (*Euphorbia horrida*) are the largest I have seen in any garden. They are native to South Africa and form huge bristly clumps nearly three feet across and tall. He has masses of clumping *Euphorbia resinifera*, a historic plant native to Morocco and used medicinally for at least two thousand years. They have spread to the point where they cannot be moved.

I found it a treat to see how the containerized stock was set out in such tight multiple rows, like *Aeonium* 'Zwartkop' placed next to a mass of yellow-flowering purple pancake cacti with a pale pink kalanchoe, a gray toothy agave, and a pudgy Easter lily cactus that resembles clusters of watermelons. His arrangement of stock in balanced juxtapositions allows the various forms to take on their own design attributes—Newcomber is a designer and maybe doesn't know it. Those who are bitten by the cactus bug and make a living servicing their bug often refuse to separate the business from the fascination. Strolling across row after row of exotic succulents aglow in the Southern California light, I sense the Eden—or to use Carl Jung's term, the *numinosum*—that is the fading essence of California.

Aloes grow best along the Southern California coast, and Serra has multitudes of the giant tree aloe (*Aloe bainesii*). It is fast growing, and from a distance full-grown plants look like eucalyptus

Fruiting specimen of the Arizona fishook barrel (*Ferocactus wislizenii*).

116 *Serra Gardens, Malibu*

Shrubby *cleistocactus*; background: propagating
area that looks more like a garden; right immediate
background are milk barrel euphorbias.

Foreground: *Agave americana mediopicta* 'Alba'; behind: *A. franzosenii*.

Most of the specimens are sold directly out of the ground.

trees. Don has successfully crossed *A. bainesii* with a tall single-stemmed Madagascar species, *A. vaombe*. This is one of two known hybrids of the tree aloe, the other being Aloe 'Hercules.' The former deserves a hybrid name because every plant is almost eight feet tall with huge nearly thornless leaves. By using tissue culture, he propagated his entire stock of this hybrid.

One fall visit to Serra Gardens highlighted the need for greater acceptance of succulents in landscaping. Practically every year there is a brushfire somewhere in or near Malibu. This time I arrived just as great clouds of gray smoke poured out of the Santa Monica Mountains. The smoke came directly over the nursery and news reports said the blaze was headed straight for the beach a mile west of the nursery. Helicopters darted around the canyon like bumblebees while two super scoopers on loan from Canada repeatedly glided over the nursery to scoop up a load of salt water from the ocean then return to head off the fire moving

This planting could only be duplicated in
Morocco where it is native: enormous clumps
of *Euphorbia resinifera*.

straight toward us. Don asked if I wanted to stay and help water down the roofs. It did not look good, because by now we could see that the fire, which started miles inland, was fast approaching Pacific Coast Highway and the ocean. At that time, I had just purchased a new car and Don said if I did not leave in a few minutes I might not be able to leave until the fire was out, which could be days. He said the last fire burned right up to the edge of the nursery and singed some succulents (their high water content prevented them from burning). Finally, we both decided I should save my car and leave quickly since the fire department uses Don's driveway as a staging area and I would be parked in by platoons of huge fire trucks and would not being going anywhere. The next day, I learned that the fire's path turned and missed the valley.

Don and I agreed that if the fire department and the state of California required hillside homes in high fire-hazard chaparral zones to be landscaped in succulents, there would be little or no chance of firestorms incinerating homes in Southern California. The fire department certainly understands that succulents do not carry a fire the way the highly flammable eucalyptus, oak, and palm do— what other reason would they have for using the center of Serra Gardens as a staging area from which to fight the deadly Malibu fires? After a devastating fire in the San Gabriel Mountains above Pasadena where numerous expensive homes were destroyed—the firestorms incinerated every tree, shrub, and herb to unrecognizable charcoal—what remained of the once lush landscape were drooping parboiled century plants and prickly pears, many of which would regenerate. Cacti and succulents are the most fire-retardant plants in Southern California and taxpayers could be saved millions of dollars each years if there were more stringent laws requiring the use of succulents in hillside landscaping, particularly in the Southern California chaparral and scrub-oak zones.

Moorten Botanical Gardens, Palm Springs

My first visit to the Moortens' cactus gardens was one of those course-setting experiences in a thirteen-year-old's life that validated a love of cacti and the desert. Both Chester "Cactus Slim" Moorten, and his wife, Pat, were gentle and unassuming ("Cactus Slim" impressed me as a "desert rat," a term we applied to those who went it alone in the desert), yet very knowledgable about succulents. They had a nursery, actually their home, I think, and cacti were everywhere. I was in heaven. The plants I brought home are long gone, but the memories, and certainly the inspiration their encouragement gave me, burn as bright as ever.

Palm Springs is at the western edge of the Coachella Valley, part of the so-called Colorado Desert, and is snuggled against the steep, barren, rocky foothills of the San Jacinto Mountains. Being a low elevation desert, the Colorado Desert is baked to death in summer, giving the region a look of toasted desolation. However, because it is an extension of the milder Sonoran Desert, there is an abundance of plant life, much of it putting in a brief spring appearance as wildflowers. Then there are cacti, lots of cacti. George Wharton James, author of *The Wonders of the Colorado Desert*, put this long-forgotten slant on the local cacti: I once asked an old Colorado Desert prospector how many varieties of cactus he was familiar with. "By gosh," said he, "you city fellers have no idea how many kinds we got. I know every one of 'em. There's the 'Full of Stickers,' 'Stick and Stay In,' 'Stick 'em Alive,' 'Stick 'em Dead,' 'Stick and Fester Cactus,' 'The Rattlesnake's Fang Cactus'. . ." In all, he named over twenty seven kinds of cacti and could identify them by how they felt on contact. I could probably add to the list.

Cactus Slim died in 1980, and Pat, with her son Clark and grandson Jason, manage the Moorten Botanic Garden, now a part of Palm Springs' colorful history. Much of the desert garden look of this playground to the stars is a credit to the Moortens' influence and their ready willingness to share their knowledge of the desert and desert plants. Actually, the 2.5-acre botanic garden and accompanying home was not purchased until 1958, and, yet today the gardens are visited by 25,000 tourists each year.

Chester "Cactus Slim" Moorten was known as the tallest and thinnest actor in Hollywood, playing opposite some of the greatest stars in the 1930s, such as Ronald Coleman, Gloria Swanson, and Greta Garbo. Pat said, "Slim was famous in Hollywood as a contortionist"; then she went on to describe some

One of the garden entrances that leads to the unexpected.

123

of the pretzel poses. Listening to how he could wrap his legs around his own neck made my back go out. Also, he was one of Mack Sennett's Keystone Cops, no doubt the thinnest one. "Cactus Slim was in the last of the silents and the first of the talkies," Pat said. By 1936, he had tired of Hollywood and settled in what is now Joshua Tree National Park. At that time he began to make a living salvaging cacti, ocotillos, and yuccas that were being torn up for road building and other construction, thus becoming an early desert-plant conservationist.

Pat Moorten came to Southern California in 1938 and worked in a cactus nursery in Beverly Hills. The owner discouraged her from working with cactus, saying it was not a woman's work. Undaunted, she pestered him until he gave in and hired her. She studied botany and landscaping at UCLA and helped lay out the Bullard Memorial Cactus Garden in Beverly Hills Park, which was designed by landscape architect Ralph Cornell, a frequent visitor to the Huntington Desert Garden.

After the Moortens were married, they moved to Palm Springs and started a florist and wedding chapel business. They had a third business, a successful cactus nursery and landscape business that survives today as a small cactus nursery, serving the tourists who stop by to walk through the botanic gardens. Through landscaping, the Moortens reconnected to Hollywood by landscaping the stars' desert retreats. Cactus gardens were designed and planted for the homes of Walt Disney, Frank Sinatra, Phil Harris, Bing Crosby, and Red Skelton. The projects were not all residential, however; in the 1970's they landscaped the original version of Living Desert Wildlife and Animal Park.

Today the Moorten Botanical Gardens is a remarkable display of 1,500 species of cacti and succulents from all over the world packed into the neatly maintained 2.5-acre grounds. It is cleverly designed with a single meandering path that leads through an enclosed Tulgey Wood (à la Lewis Carroll) of strange and bizarre cactus shapes that look like they might talk—or worse. The garden is not as old as the Huntington; it opened in 1958, but the specimens have grown to full maturity with plants that tolerate one of the hottest and driest deserts. The light shade provided by palo verde and other desert trees, nicely placed contortionist-shaped boulders, dead tree trunks, and competely fossilized tree trunks gives the place a charm often exceeding that of the Huntington. Whether it be intentional or unintentional, the garden was designed to fascinate and enchant through the suggestive imagery of the Sonoran Desert.

Most of the plants are cacti, yuccas, ocotillos, and desert trees native to Mexico, including Baja California. The cacti of Baja are important components of the garden. In 1950 the Moortens drove their 1929 Buick down the Baja peninsula. Many of the specimens in the garden are from their collecting trips to Mexico. The garden signage is imaginative, casually hand-lettered plant names on old weathered pieces of wood—a nice Disneyesque feature. Pat's son, Clark, who manages the garden and small nursery, proudly points out an enormous prized specimen of elephant tree (*Bursera microphylla*), found in Baja. Old Baja hands say this particular specimen, with its twenty-foot spread, is the largest seen in or out of cultivation. There is no plant record-keeping system as such, but both Pat Moorten and her son can tell much about the collections, and there are plenty of stories about harrowing experiences in the desert in search of cacti. The path leads to a display greenhouse, called the Cactarum, set down a couple of feet below ground, which saved on construction costs and gives the structure something of a natural cooling system. Instead of benches, there are raised planter beds in the center and along the sides, an interesting feature not seen today in greenhouse design. Among the specimens are two welwitschias, acquired from the botanical collection of the late Gil Tegelberg, Jr., a highly respected grower. The welwitschias do very well here, a bit surprising considering the low desert humidity. Outside the greenhouse is a colorful display of pincushion cacti planted Huntington-like among red volcanic rock. Clark Moorten says the garden has experienced winter temperatures down to a deadly 15 degrees Fahrenheit and in the summer as high as 128 degrees, which would do serious damage to an unprotected garden and anyone who attempted to care for it. The botanic garden is a valuable resource and living reference book for local residents seeking to know what grows best in this area.

Inside the Cactarum showing
unusual barrel cacti.

The Moortens were influential in the Cactus and Succulent Society of America, working to put on plant exhibits and national conventions; likewise, they were founding members of the California Cactus Grower's Association, of which Clark is president. The special emphasis on succulents native to Mexico is a reflection of the Moortens' many expeditions to Mexico, some with another pioneering nurseryman, Howard Gates, the first collector to drive to the southernmost tip of Baja and back in a car. He accomplished this feat in the 1920s when there was no real road and when more time was spent on auto repair than on fieldwork. Other traveling companions included Dr. George Lindsay, former director of the California Academy of Sciences and authority on my favorite barrel cacti, the genus *Ferocactus*.

What makes a visit to the Moorten Botanical Gardens fascinating for the plant enthusiast is discovering many mystery plants that Clark thinks may be new-but-never-described species collected by his parents. I was amazed to see a twenty-foot tree of the giant candelabra cactus of central Mexico, a pitahaya (*Stenocereus weberi*). A specimen of this kind at the Huntington was Hertrich's favorite cactus; he would be pleased to see this robust and healthy flowering one. This cactus has all but disappeared from cultivation but would make a most impressive accent in the home landscape. Another mystery plant is almost lost in a tangle shrubby cacti. It is a very rare dwarf form of the Arizona organ pipe cactus, but this form, *Stenocereus thurberi* var. *littoralis*, is not found in Arizona, but rather near the tip of Baja California. The stem tips were garlanded with clusters of delicate rose pink funnel-shaped flowers. A further mystery plant is a Myrtillocactus unofficially named in honor of their good friend Gil Tegelberg.

The garden is within walking distance of downtown Palm Springs. The best time to see it is in the spring, especially from mid-April to early May when the cacti, and everything else in the desert, is in flower. The garden's nicely shaded botanical cactus display is complemented by a verdant lawn in front of the house and is contrasted by a single palm tree with a painfully contorted trunk that makes me think of Cactus Slim. Clark says it is the backdrop for weddings. A cactus garden is one of Palm Springs' most popular wedding chapels.

About 1954, Walt Disney asked the Moortens to meet him in Anaheim to discuss a landscape project. Pat Moorten said they drove up to a packing shed in an orange grove and were puzzled by the sign atop the shed: it read: "Disneyland." Walt was inside and asked if they would landscape what he intended to call the Living Desert, which is of course what they did best. I like to think of Walt Disney as a friend to deserts and to cacti.

Previous page: Clark Moorten's favorite cacti are the hedgehogs (*echinocereus*).

Living Desert Wildlife and Animal Park, Palm Desert

Living Desert Wildlife and Animal Park can be described as a New Age zoo. Walking or hiking along its six miles of weaving paths and trails gives a sense of being in a natural habitat, or biome, where animals like cheetahs, zebras, and Arabian oryx are more at home than the visitors. The animals are not displayed on small, over-designed stages, as in many urban zoos; the park's nearly 2,000-acre size and purpose confirm its biological reserve status. Living Desert is both an accredited zoo and botanical garden, like San Diego's Wild Animal Park. It is filled with numerous desert-adapted plant displays and gardens that serve educational and community functions beyond those of a traditional zoo. In fact, the community role almost puts the park in a class by itself.

Part of the Living Desert lies within a desert wash, one of many that drain from the mountains bordering the Coachella Valley. Its context is the driest of the North American deserts, the Colorado Desert, a drier and hotter extension of the Sonoran Desert. The irony is that this desert is only forty or fifty miles from the Mojave Desert, which enjoys a higher elevation and a bit more rainfall. The Colorado Desert extends to the Colorado River 150 miles to the east, where it becomes the much milder Arizona Sonoran Desert, which is wetter and has summer rainfall. In the washes of the Colorado Desert are billowy Smoke trees (*Dalea*, or *Psorothamnus, spinosa*) with their indigo blue pea-like flowers strangely heralding the onset of summer. Other adaptees include the creosote bush (*Larrea divaricata*), various species of mesquite, and the famous California Desert fan palm (*Washingtonia filifera*), the signature tree for nearby Palm Springs and any other community in the Coachella Valley that has palm in its name. The palms are not found just anywhere; they occur at natural oases and seeps in the surrounding rocky desert foothills, where they still grow wild. Some believe the palms once lined the shore of the not-so-ancient Lake Cahuilla, which dried up in the fifteenth century, possibly due to a change in the Colorado River drainage. The Cahuilla Indians could have planted some of the palms. It is thought that the Cahuillas' use of the Desert agave (*Agave deserti*) for food affected its distribution. The Cahuilla Indians once depended upon the desert fan palm for building materials and food and it is among the dominant plantings at Living Desert.

The importance of palms is reflected in the Living Desert's palm garden, where there are nearly a dozen cultivars of the date palm (*Phoenix dactylifera*), introduced to the Coachella Valley as a

Salvaged saguaros reestablished and thriving at the Park. Brittlebush (*Encelia farinosa*) is a popular component of southwest landscapes.

133

The Johnson Cactus Garden; beyond is the
Wortz Demonstration Garden.

successful agricultural crop at the beginning of the twentieth century. Date culture has all but disappeared from this part of the desert; much of the industry that gave the Colorado Desert an agricultural economy and its oasis appeal has now been transplanted to the lush, tropical illusions surrounding Las Vegas casinos.

A zoo tour at Living Desert is more like a botanic garden tour, because its designers and staff recognize the important role of plants in animal survival. The park plays a role in the local community through its skillfully designed demonstration gardens, a full-service and beautifully maintained nursery with an enviable selection of plants (including desert-adapted cacti and succulents) for home xeriscaping, and several specialty gardens and collections.

Dave Heveron, plant collections manager, says the Living Desert's gardens are maintained by six full-time gardeners and two plant propagators who work in the facility's nursery, where plants are grown to be planted in the zoo. The public nursery has a staff of three. Dave's Living Desert horticulture program fosters community support not only by making many desert-adapted plants available to civic landscape projects, but also through a desert plant salvage program, whereby cacti and yuccas are routinely rescued from the path of construction projects and their bulldozers. One such project is successfully conducted in Yucca Valley, where the city notifies Living Desert of areas scheduled for road expansions, utility right of ways, and any major planned subdivisions. Dave visits the site and selects plants suitable for rescuing, then transplants them to the zoo's landscape. This project has added to the gardens numerous pencil chollas, compass barrels, hedgehog cacti, and yuccas, including Joshua trees. Dave gives the reestablishment success rate as 30 percent—a lot better than when the plants are left to die in a landfill. He has the most trouble transplanting wild Joshua trees and thinks they are not suited to the low elevation (about 400 feet above sea level); possibly it does not get cold enough in the winter. The problem is that wild Joshua trees survive captivity little better than many animals captured in the wild. Probably the best strategy is to plant seed-grown plants from containers and give them water during the scorching summer, which, ironically, is what Wilson Popenoe claimed about a hundred years ago would make date culture a success in the Coachella Valley—water and heat.

There are at least eighteen specialized gardens at Living Desert, plus landscapes connected to animal exhibits, and they are generally classified as either geographic, such as the Vizcaino Garden (Baja, California); taxonomic, such as the barrel cactus and

prickly pear gardens; educational, such as the popular hummingbird Garden or the Cahuilla Ethnobotany Garden; or demonstration, such as the Wortz Demonstration Garden and the Johnston Cactus Garden. All the gardens are landscaped and labeled to allow the public—including 25,000 schoolchildren yearly—to learn about the value of desert and dryland vegetation, not only for animal and human survival, but also of for beauty and for conservation.

The Wortz Demonstration Garden, strategically situated next to the plant nursery, is an exceptional tour de force of bold rockwork. It was designed and installed by Wayne Conner and Living Desert nursery manager Glenn Huntington. There are eye-catching undulating terraces planted with agaves and cacti, mixed with Southwest native shrubs and herbaceous perennials. Accents include saguaro and ocotillo. Shade is provided by ironwood trees (*Olneya tesota*), a Sonoran Desert native, and fast-growing yellow-flowered palo verde trees (*Parkinsonia aculeata*) that are naturalized throughout the grounds. For a cooling element, there is a sunken pond, nearly concealed by large, flat, angular stones. The rockwork is phenomenal and the garden should be considered a major contribution to residential desert landscaping. The rock size—some are large boulders—and rusty color nicely balance with the model residence and pleasantly harmonize with the plantings.

Also within view of the nursery is the Johnston Cactus Garden, a small but effectively landscaped demonstration garden with many kinds of tough North American cacti, including the Arizona saguaro (*Carnegiea gigantea*). The saguaro is the treelike branched cactus most commonly associated with the Arizona Sonoran Desert and now more popular than ever in desert landscaping from Las Vegas to Palm Springs. The garden is contoured with granite-cobble mulched raised beds. Heveron occasionally acquires important cactus and other plant collections for the continually expanding Living Desert collection. He has, as does the Huntington and other botanic gardens, an accessioning system and keeps planting and plant-evaluation records.

The palm collection is relevant to cactus gardening, because they are associated with desert biomes throughout the world. I observed several species of brahea palm thriving in desert

areas in Mexico. They grew among century plants, prickly pear cacti, and bromeliads. Desert palms are components of the Huntington's landscape, and their usefulness as accents or background plantings should not be overlooked. According to Heveron, the palm collection includes nine or so cultivars of the date palm (*Phoenix dactylifera*), presumably those most popular in the Coachella Valley date industry. At one time there were about two dozen date palm cultivars, introduced here about 1910 by the U.S. Bureau of Plant Introduction from plantations in Algeria and the Persian Gulf.

It is difficult to tour the botanical zoological park without encountering unusual succulents. The African Savanna is planted with aloes that miraculously survive the more than 120-degree summer heat and the dry winter. The many aloes that have survived are a credit to the very capable horticulture staff, which has no trouble growing outdoors the impala lily (*Adenium obesum*), a succulent oleander relative. In addition to succulents are many associated plants, such as the twenty-four species of African acacias that give an unparalleled authentic effect to the zoo's African section. These acacias, like the monkey thorn (*Acacia galpinii*) and the white thorn (*A. albida*), are associated with the dry African savannas, where many have a flat-top look. This flat-top character is rarely seen in plants grown outside their natural habitat. The flat-top look is absent in the Living Desert too, but these acacias make more robust and attractive specimens than those at the much milder-climate Huntington.

The nursery offers for sale a variety of cacti and succulents, most of them growing in the Living Desert's gardens. Also available for purchase are palo verde, Mexican bird of paradise (*caesalpinia*) and other beautiful flowering legumes; agaves, beargrass, and yuccas; and perennials such as evening primrose, desert sages, and ornamental grasses. All the perennials work well with cacti and succulents. This sort of plant-introduction program where inventory is closely linked to the specialty and demonstration gardens is a much-discussed but seldom-enacted concept. Living Desert is living proof that plant introduction to the community is a great contribution to gardening and landscaping and I hope it will be imitated by other botanic gardens.

Overleaf: Naturalistic desert thorn scrub
scene with palmillas (*Yucca elata*).

O'Neill Garden, San Juan Capistrano

The O'Neill cactus and drought-tolerant garden is sculpted with well-grown cacti and succulents, California natives, and other dryland herbaceous perennials. The garden's natural scenery frames magnificent views of the historic Rancho Mission Viejo. In 1979, Donna O'Neill asked that I design a cactus garden at their ranch home. At the time I was unfamiliar with the ranch and was puzzled at the absence of neighbors—only endless miles of oak woodland. Donna told me that the ranch was large, really large—about 30,000 acres.

Rancho Mission Viejo, also known as the O'Neill Ranch, was part of the much larger Rancho Santa Margarita y Flores, owned by three generations of O'Neills. Richard O'Neill arrived in San Francisco from New York in 1850 and opened a slaughter house. He believed there was more money to be made selling sides of beef than digging for gold. He was right, and in 1880 he used the profits to purchase beef cattle to put on ranch land he acquired from John Forester, an English sailor who married the sister of Pio Pico, the first governor of California. Here he could raise his own meat supply and ship beef from nearby Dana Point and San Diego to San Francisco in as little as seventeen hours.

Prior to the O'Neill purchase of the land, the ranch was part of mission lands confiscated by the government of Mexico in the 1830s and initially acquired by Pio Pico. The ranch was—and to a great extent still is—a world unto itself, generating its own cultural gravity. It extended along some twenty miles of Southern California coastline and was about the size of Rhode Island, about 270,000 acres, or two and one-half times the size of the San Fernando Valley. Its immense size allowed for diversification into citrus and other crops, and parcels were leased out to farmers. Today there are 700 head of cattle, far less than the original 16,000; citrus groves; and five large plant nurseries, which serve the landscape industry throughout Southern California. Among them is Mike Evans's Tree of Life nursery, twenty acres and 400 species of California natives, the largest supplier in the state.

Part of the garden first planted in 1979; view looking north across spacious ranch lands.

Overleaf: right center : mature *Agave parryi* var. *truncata*; further right: blue barrel cacti (*Ferocactus glaucescens*). Across right : *Agave horrida*.

The O'Neill cactus garden begins at the edge of a green lawn, and from the living room one sees flowering aloes, columnar cacti, and glowing golden barrels. The primary focal point is a rare and spectacular multibranched aztec column cactus (*Neobuxbaumia polylopha*). This is related to the old man cactus of Mexico and resembles an assemblage of green pillars. Around the Aztec column are several large golden barrel cacti that make an eye-catching composition. A graveled path leads downhill to a colony of robust and flowering pipe organ cactus specimens (*Pachycereus marginatus*) and a gigantic grayish mound of yellow-flowering silver dollar prickly pear (*Opuntia robusta*) with oversized round pads. Like many prickly pear cacti, its fruits are edible.

The garden is planted with a variety of agave species, most notably the giants too large for most private gardens or collections. Here there is ample room for them, and some are planted in open spaces as sturdy dramatic accents resembling sculpted bronzes set against the distant, open oak parkland. *Agave mapisaga var. lisa* is a classic pulque agave from the highlands of central Mexico, and its origins may go back to prehistoric times. When fully grown it is over sixteen feet in diameter and the treelike inflorescence with its hundreds of nectiferous flowers will tower twenty to thirty feet above the plant. This agave offsets and eventually forms a thicket. It has the perfect home here at the ranch.

Farther downhill the garden features ample plantings of salvias, shasta daisies, manzanita, buckweat, Ceanothus, and Cistus. These combine to create a beautiful meadow effect with some of Donna O'Neill's favorite plants and represent a collaboration between Donna and landscape architect Lynne Deane Barbaro of Newport Beach. Lynne designed a low rock wall next to the drive, and expert plantsman Roger Weld tucked in stonecrops and the native chalk plant (*Dudleya pulverulenta*), making a perfect environment for the soft-leaf succulents. Lynne quickly learned that Donna likes walking into the garden, getting a sense of what plant looks good where, and not drawing up plans. If the plant does not fit, it is moved. Here, the designer's principal tool is the pick and shovel.

Both the landscape and the many botanical surprises throughout the garden are tributes to Donna's sharp eye for stimulating combinations of form and texture plus her love of experimentation. Like a true horticulturist, she does not hesitate to

Silver dollar prickly pear (*Opuntia robusta*) in bristly bud.

push the envelope—to succeed with something mysterious, unknown, or untried, such as the karoo acacia, or the ocotillo-like *Alluadia procera*, a Madagascar endemic. She loves the scented-leaved salvias and desert acacias. One them is the perfume acacia (*Acacia caven*); its fragrance in late afternoon and evening drifts into the O'Neill livingroom and enlivens the senses. She has demonstrated an uncanny sense of the correct plant form and texture for each portion of the "yard." What she achieved is an exotic cactus garden that spatially metamorphoses into a native and xerophyte garden and that, away from the residence, fades into the ranch's indigenous coastal sage scrub and oak woodland biome.

Euphorbias grow very well on the hillside. The Hercules club (*Euphorbia canariensis*) forms a dramatic cascade, as it would in its steep, rocky Canary Island habitat. It has perfect exposure and none of the territorial restrictions that keep many shrubby euphorbias from achieving their full landscape potential. There are milk-barrel euphorbias (*Euphorbia horrida*) and the densely shrubby blue euphorbia (*E. coerulescens*) that in South Africa forms thickets so large and so dense that they are important protective habitats for smaller mammals.

The silvery-leaved yuccas that look like bottlebrushes are *Yucca thompsoniana*, common to the Sonoran and Chihuahuan deserts. In April, they send up long-stalked clusters of white flowers that last through early summer. Unlike agaves, the yuccas, with one exception, do not die after flowering. The one single species that does die is a California native, the white-flowered Lord's candle (*Y. whipplei*), which usually forms a solitary rosette of over one hundred stiff, dagger-like leaves that give hikers in the local foothills memorable jabs in the shins; it lives about ten or twelve years and sends up a thick treelike inflorescence just like a century plant. The enormous flower stalks, a familiar sight in May in the Southern California foothills, develop to maturity in only ten days. If you grow one in a Southern California garden and let it go to seed, the following year there may be seedlings and promise of further displays. I noted an absence of fruit on the Thompson yucca, meaning that the pollinator, the pronuba moth, was not in the vicinity. Research suggests yucca species may be pollinated only by a species of moth specially adapted to it.

Turning a corner downhill one finds specimen night-blooming cerei—actually some unusual and unnamed hydrids from Dave Grigsby's Nursery in Vista, which some consider the world

center of the cactus-growing industry. We also find flashy flowering *Lobivia* 'Glorious,' and a soft pink flowering mass of *Euphorbia xantii*. There are, as well, garambullo cacti (*myrtillocactus*) with edible fruits the size of gooseberries; early summer becomes feast time for birds as the sweet fleshy fruits ripen and split open.

Farther downhill are more plantings of large pulque agaves, along with many colorful prickly pears, columnar cacti, and yuccas. The agave and prickly pears in the garden and elsewhere on the ranch are apt themes, for nearby are the historic El Camino Real and the San Juan Capistrano Mission. The prevalence of these plants suggests the Hispanic influences of a bygone era. Aloes are among the O'Neills' favorites. Donna loves the flowers, especially the tall candelabra aloes, such as *Aloe ferox*, and the masses of the canary yellow flowering medicinal aloe, *A. vera*.

The portion of the cactus garden planted nearest the residence features not only the golden barrels, but also several smaller agaves, such as the Queen Victoria century plant (*Agave victoriae reginae*), the longest lived of the agaves: from twenty to forty-five years. The name century plant was applied by the British to their potted specimens overwintered in heated greenhouses then placed out doors for a short, cool summer. Under these conditions, a flowering century plant was rare; if one did manage to flower, it was a newsworthy event. Someone's offhanded comment that agaves take a century to flower was a bit of misinformation absorbed by the public. Most agaves in "semitropical" California flower in seven to thirty-five years, depending on the species. All but a very few flower within twenty-five years.

There are also splendid clumps of several kinds of pincushion cacti, which thrive on the hilltop exposure. The ranch is near enough to the ocean that despite the bright afternoon sunlight the pincushion cacti do not burn. Amazingly, a planting of bishop's cap cactus (*Astrophytum myriostigma*) is still thriving twenty years after being planted.

The cactus and succulent landscape of golden barrels, Aztec column, and showy agaves is interplanted with groundcovers of reddish-leaved succulents, including *Crassula* 'Camp Fire' and *Sedum rubrotinctum*. Once again the ocean air permits even more delicate stonecrops to tolerate full afternoon sun. In hot inland gardens they cook in the summer heat and frequent waterings and afternoon shade are indispensable for their survival. Herbaceous succulents in the stonecrop or crassula family normally are not long lived, but

O'Neill Garden, San Juan Capistrano 147

these, plus the fuzzy-leaved Echeveria 'Doris Taylor' tucked beneath stones have thrived in the O'Neill garden for over eighteen years.

Striking natural geometries are displayed in the blue-ribbed bristly yellow-spined *Notocactus magnificus*, a native to Brazil that has bright yellow flowers. It is usually grown in pots and displayed at cactus shows, but none look as magnificent as the O'Neills' plants. Similar in look, but native to Mexico, is the blue barrel (*Ferocactus glaucescens*), but it has stouter spines and eventually forms large golden-spined mounds. This globular cactus does best with a little afternoon shade; it will take decades to grow into a clump two or three feet across. The creeping devil cactus (*Stenocereus eruca*) grows flat on the ground, and its long, caterpillar-like stems have formed a network of horizontal branching among the obese golden barrel cacti.

Do not accept as gospel everything you read in books about what can and cannot be grown in specific regions; hard-and-fast rules cannot possibly take into account all permutations of climate, soil, exposure, and expertise. Always experiment. I had doubts that an uncommon specimen of Peruvian old woman cactus (*Espostoa melanostele*) would survive outdoors because of cold winters, but was amazed to see that the O'Neill's have grown a multibranched plant for twenty years.

The ranch recently established a 1,200-acre nature reserve, called the O'Neill Ranch Conservancy. Laura Cohen, conservancy director, says the reserve contains one of the last watersheds in coastal Southern California that is not a cemented channel or has a dam. Here there is one of the largest, if not the largest, coast live oak (*Quercus agrifolia*) in California. Its trunk diameter is nearly eight feet, and the crown diameter is over one hundred feet. This behemoth, which Laura Cohen calls the 'Mother Oak,' could be six to eight hundred years old. Nearby in a creek bed are California sycamore (*Platanus racemosa*) groves that could be a thousand years old or more. There are several endangered plant and animal species found within the conservancy. The Conservancy features a number of wildflower and wildlife walks, stargazing, and school projects. In 1769, the Portola Expedition tramped through this part of the ranch, camped, and must have been consumed by Southern California's golden glow, which does today for the human spirit what gold nuggets did for the Argonauts of '49.

Beautiful specimens of *Agave horrida* and a very rare form of Aztec Column (*Neobuxbaumia polylopha*). Native coast live oak (*Quercus agrifolia*) in background.

Patrick Anderson Garden, Fallbrook

Patrick Anderson, a loyal Huntington garden volunteer, gardens at his home in hilly north San Diego County. His cactus and succulent garden is a work in progress, presently covering a half-acre slope once covered with lime trees and looking down on his ranch-style house with its red-tiled roof. One enters his property, along a gently curved drive bordered by a double row of Peruvian pepper trees. The Peruvian pepper tree (*Shinus molle*), first introduced at the San Diego Mission about 1835 by an American sailor, is so identified with the California landscape that it is often called the California pepper tree. Here they are living on borrowed time, for Patrick's love of succulents and exotic xerophytes is overthrowing his original, leafier, landscape. The hillside cactus garden is only the beginning in the transformation of his property to a succulent garden.

The cactus garden evolved from a childhood interest in succulents and a neighbor's generosity in sharing cuttings. Patrick grew up in San Gabriel, near both the Huntington and the San Gabriel Mission. He is an avid student of European gardens and garden history (there is little evidence of that in the cactus garden). A dedicated Huntington Plant Sale volunteer and a board member the San Diego Horticultural Society, his exuberant love of plants is reflected in the often-startling combinations of succulents in conjunction with the extensive use of stone and metal sculpture accents. Everywhere there are pleasing compositions and plant juxtapositions, particularly the winter flowering aloes and mesembs in a hillside setting, one that certainly makes full use of the coral aloe (*A. striata*) for dramatic effect.

Patrick has developed bright plantings of golden barrels, aeoniums, yuccas, pipe organ cacti, and a fierce specimen of the giant *Furcraea macdougallii*. Here one sees the designer's eye, particularly in the use of a textured flagstone called Desert Bark and in the incorporation of metal sculptures. Here even more-common plants can make an exotic display, such as the so-called gopher plant, *Euphorbia rigida*, which is planted and naturalized to the extent that its bluish-leaved mounds are unifying elements. Near his pavilion is a beautifully laid out display of golden barrels; elsewhere are softer compositions of bushy aeoniums; there are wispy yellow-flowered bulbines, similar to, but softer than, aloes. Eye-catching variegated agaves punctuate the greener plantings. The colonnaded pipe organ cactus and saguaro-like pasacana cactus (*Trichocereus pasacana*) give the garden both height and structure. Splashes of rich oranges provided by plantings of Lampranthus 'Gold Nugget' prove that ice-plant groundcovers can be used as accent spots of color with just two or three manageable plants tucked here and there between rocks rather than always planted in blinding sheets of blazing color. Dymmondia, an unusual ground-hugging groundcover related to the genus *Gazania*, spreads over the rocks like a spilled can of gray paint.

Aloes are the major feature in the garden; rather than a tidal wave of species there is a careful selection of those that are effective and can be seen from the pavilion. The pavilion grew from a simple gazebo to the present permanent and solidly constructed structure, which, with its red-tiled roof echoes the residence. Patrick says the pavilion is his refuge, where he can enjoy the garden.

The point has been made that aloes are one of the best sources of winter color in Southern California. Rarely, if ever, does it become cold enough (except in the desert) to freeze the flowers. If temperatures drop below 28 degrees Fahrenheit for most of the night, the flowers will freeze. If it gets that cold in my

Metal urn planted with a curous combination of succulents including *Pachyphytum oviferum*, *Echeveria gibbiflora*, *euphorbia*, and *sedum*.

Overleaf: Hillside garden showing pavilion; below left: verbena, mission cactus; Pasacana cactus; below right and far right, variegated agaves.

garden, I cover the smaller aloes and other plants with sheets, burlap bags, or carpeting. Patrick's garden is nearly frost free. Some notable aloes that do well for him are the sentry-like *Aloe marlothii* with its huge candelabras of yellow or orange flowers. This aloe does not branch; it grows to fifteen feet and is used either as an accent or as a background, but here is placed so that its magnificent winter floral display can be enjoyed. This hillside setting is perfect for this aloe. A related species, but more earthbound, is *A. petricola* with thick grayish leaves. Though smaller, it grows more slowly and throws a few offsets over a period of many years. The bright two-tone, forked inflorescence consists of crimson buds and contrasting creamy yellow-white flowers.

Other aloes that contribute differing effects are *A. capitata* from Madagascar, named for its orange heads of flowers, and *A. suprafoliata* from South Africa, to me this provides the brightest, cheeriest flowers for the Christmas holidays. Also noted for its color is the coral aloe (*A. striata*) and an unnamed vigorous hybrid. Both are red flowering and long lasting. The beauty of the coral aloe is that it is thornless. The most impressive plant in the garden is Patrick's *Aloe* 'Hercules'. As the name suggests, it is a giant, actually a cross between the great tree aloe (*A. bainesii*) and the quiver tree (*A. dichotoma*). 'Hercules' has indications of hybrid vigor, meaning eventually it might be the giant sequoia of the garden.

The hillside cactus garden is young, begun only four years ago. It seems much older, a credit to a keen eye for what looks best with what plant and what rock. Patrick is the designer; his design implements are plants and shovel, not pencil and paper. He takes little credit for his plantscaping: "Mine is a garden of happy accidents," he says. It still takes an eye; he is an avid horticulturist, researching the characteristics of each new species in his library, learning how each grows and flowers, and keeping computer inventories and records, including evaluations of how the plants perform in his garden. What amazes me is how little water is used in the garden. Patrick rarely waters and during the summer only once every three weeks. My own garden gets weekly hot-weather waterings, but I have a sandy soil with little clay; Patrick's soil is heavier, and the light and humidity are different. He does have one problem, namely ants, which have taken up ranching aphids in the crowns of his aloes, causing damage to the growth tip that forces unnatural branching. He takes it in stride, saying the ants help propagate his plants. It is always nice to have help in the garden.

Expert rockwork for smaller succulents; above: *Aloe peglerae* and *Echeveria* 'Pinky.'

Below left foreground *Aloe ciliaris*, thriving
yellow-flowered *Euphorbia rigida*; far right:
Aloe arborescens; *echium*, aloes and agave
cover the hill.

Phil Favel Garden, Escondido

Nestled in a remote ranchy area near Escondido in San Diego Country, Phil Favel's garden is a symphonic cacophony of weird succulents that departs from the conventional lush trees, shrubs, bluegrass lawns, and horse stables of the surrounding area. Elfin Forest is off the beaten track in north San Diego County and Favel's garden is well concealed until one enters the narrow aloe-lined drive and is hit visually by a landscape straight out of Namaqualand. As one goes up the drive, which traverses a rise that drops precipitously on both sides, the eye is overwhelmed by three and a half acres of aloes, agaves, cacti, and bizarre exotic trees. In January, dozens of yellow- and coral-flowered *Aloe microstigma* fill a nearby slope. Phil is perhaps the most passionate aloe collector I know, and he has the space, the hilly exposure, and the climate to grow one of the largest aloe assemblages in the world.

Out of 450 aloe species described by scientists, Phil has 300 growing in his garden and knows the botany of each and every one. Twelve years ago, he began his garden from seeds and cuttings, many from the Huntington, where he is a regular visitor. He can look at any one of his thousands of plants, give its scientific name, name the collector, and where and when it was collected or obtained. There are no labels—his database is in his head. Many species in his garden are rarely, if ever, seen outside their habitat. Others are so new they are undescribed. He refers to his undescribed species by the name of the locality where they were first discovered; for example, the Rhadwa Aloe, discovered at Rhadwa, Yemen by Sheila Colenette, aloe expert and author of *An Illustrated Guide to the Flowers of Saudi Arabia*. When the species description is published, it will be named *Aloe porphyrostachys*, for its brilliant red colors. Phil does his own traveling in search of aloes, ferreting out old, new, and long-lost species from remote deserts. He has been to Africa, Madagascar, and Yemen seeking the rare and the unusual. Often he finds relatively common species, but in regions where they have not been documented; this adds to knowledge of the species' distribution in the wild and the information is eagerly shared with other aloe lovers.

Species aloes, Southern Hemisphere succulents, usually flower in our winter—December through March. The aloes seldom adjust to the seasons; thankfully so because their spikes of brightly colored flowers are a cheery relief to our short and often gloomy days. However, not all aloes follow the rule, and among Phil's thousands of aloes there are flowers every day of the year. His favorites are planted either on the hillside below the house or close to the drive, so they are always in full view. Especially spectacular is the planting of the kokerboom, or quiver tree (*A. dichotoma*), from Namaqualand in South Africa. Their weird, inverted-cone-shaped trunks with stubby forked branches eerily dot the stony hillside. First discovered in 1685 by Dutch explorer Simon Van Der Stel, *A. dichotoma* has been a favorite among succulent collectors all over the world. It has taken three hundred years for nurseries to be willing to grow it to a size worthy of using in the landscape. The Huntington recently acquired some of these to plant in the newly renovated African section. Ironically, the nursery that finally grew them to specimen size for local gardens, Western Cactus Growers, is just a few miles from Phil Favel's garden. For all its strangeness, *A. dichotoma* is a striking accent plant and is right at home on the well-drained sunny hillside. It flowers in our fall, and is covered with showy canary yellow blossoms on short stalks.

It would take a monograph to comment on all the species in the Favel garden. It is clear from the mass plantings that those with colorful reddish bronzed leaves, like *A. dorotheae*, *A. ukambensis*, *A. vanbalenii*, and *A. morogoroensis* are preferred for their fiery accent effect. These aloes—all East African species—are eye-catchers without the flowers. Only *A. vanbalenii* is grown for landscaping; the others are grown for potted greenhouse collections. *A. ukambensis* is quite rare in cultivation and seldom offered in the trade. Bright sunlight, drought, and cold are the various conditions responsible for activating the reddish leaf pigments. Too much shade, water, or fertilizer will greatly diminish the intensity of the leaf color.

A most impressive display is a mass planting of *A. rubroviolacea*, creeping over a slope below the house. Because Phil is networked with aloe enthusiasts throughout the world, even one in Scotland, he thinks he has every imaginable form of this

The graceful *Aloe thraskii* of Kwazulu Natal; background flowering *A. cameronii*.

species, and a great many others. As a true collector he has developed a sharp eye for unusual forms that are at variance with the botanical description of the species. For those who think *A. rubroviolacea* is commonplace, there are his plantings of the newly discovered species *A. pseudorubroviolacea*. Many gardeners and collectors regard both species as among the showiest in the genus. There are forests of bulky and tall *A. ferox*, *A. marlothii*, and *A. spectabilis*, all with large candelabra-like inflorescences of red, orange, yellow, and white flowers. He has every color phase of these species, including white-flowered forms. Though the Huntington may have more aloe species, not to mention a couple hundred hybrids, Favel's aloe kingdom is unsurpassed for its massive display of species in numerous documented variant forms, vital to a conservation collection.

Three and a half acres of aloes needs relief, and fortunately Phil provides it with some very unusual trees, such as the baobab—perhaps the one of the few growing in the U.S. outside the Florida tropics. The baobab (*Adansonia digitata*) grows across much of sub-Saharan Africa, but tolerates no frost. Saint-Exupéry's Little Prince would probably want to talk to Phil about baobabs. Another oddity is the Socotran fig (*Ficus socotrana*) endemic to a desert island off the coast of southern Arabia that has some of the most unusual plants in the world.

Lampranthus and drosanthemums, groundcover mesembs, are planted in masses on slopes around the house; the floral effect is a kaleidoscopic collage of Kool Aid pink, lilac, and red orange, relieved only by an occasional splotch of golden yellow California poppy. This display is the best argument against the use of preemergent weed killer, for these mesembs reseed themselves, ensuring a mass effect as older plants fade and die.

Farthest away from the drive is another hill of more aloes, but included here are a great many cacti native to Mexico and to the Southwest. Being a native Texan and owning a large ranch in the Big Bend region of Texas, Phil cannot shake off his first love, the cacti of the Chihuahuan Desert. He is becoming more and more interested in *echinocereus* and *thelocactus*, rather small and diminutive compared to the great mass of aloes. As I walked through the garden, I was continually cautioned not to step on them, for he had planted thousands of seedlings; in fact, some were germinating on their own in the dwarf bunch grass, just as they would do in the wild.

Echinocereus pectinatus from the Big Bend region.

Phil's garden is not landscaped in a conventional manner; it is divided into broad sections containing species with similar water, soil, and cultural needs, such as the special area he created for aloes endemic to Namibia. There is definitely a touch of wildness here as this prickly paradise is pathless. Phil—the designer and the gardener—might wish for paths when the spiny plants get bigger and he gets older. He is happy designing through creative botanical puttering. Just like the Little Prince, he has his very own asteroid and does as he pleases. Although his garden is basically a collection, its primary design element is cultural need based on light and water. Even so, Phil rarely waters or fertilizes. The well-drained soil and its diatomaceous base, the bright sun exposure, and winter rains comprise the basic maintenance strategy. I can see another mania coming: Phil revealed that he has ten thousand seedling hedgehog cacti growing in his private nursery and that he intends to plant all of them on his hillsides—perhaps as reminders of the Big Bend region. Aloes and hedgehogs? Well, it is his garden, after all.

Coppery leaved *Aloe cameronii*; full sun and limited watering gives it color. Australian bottle tree (*Brachychiton rupestre*) in background.

Spring flowering lampranthus naturalized on hillside; foreground: *Aloe rubroviolacea* from Yemen.

One of the hundreds of hedgehog cacti planted among grasses, a very natural association.

Balboa Park Cactus Gardens, San Diego

Balboa Park is next to the world famous San Diego Zoo. The 1,200-acre park is San Diego's historic showpiece, landscaped more like a botanic garden or arboretum than a park and a reflection of perhaps the most horticulturally aware city in California. The park was begun in the 1860s. By the beginning of the twentieth century it had greatly expanded and was landscaped with subtropical trees and shrubs from the nursery of pioneer San Diego horticulturist and nurserywoman Kate O. Sessions. This great nurserywoman's contribution was augmented by an enthusiastic community effort to grow and donate plant specimens to landscape Balboa Park for

the 1915 Exposition that celebrated and promoted the opening of the Panama Canal. After the exposition closed, many buildings remained and were converted to the park's many popular museums and other public attractions.

Along Park Boulevard and across from the zoo parking lot is the cactus garden. This is a relatively new garden, installed in the mid 1950s, and covers three or four acres along several hundred yards of the boulevard and fades out down a steep knoll. Many of the plants, especially agaves and aloes, are remnants of the Kate O. Sessions Agave and Aloe Garden that still exists in the park. This

Above: The newly restored Kate O. Sessions Garden

Tree euphorbia of South and eastern Africa, *Euphorbia ingens*.

Dombeya wallichii in flower.

much earlier garden was laid out in 1935 in honor of Kate Sessions and currently is being renovated. The new agave and aloe garden certainly has higher visibility and is integrated into Balboa Park's meandering system of bicycling and hiking trails.

Former Balboa Park head gardener John Paseck was responsible for exuberant aloe displays and the overall look of the garden. Undoubtedly some of the older plants have long-forgotten stories, as they came from early and historic San Diego nurseries, such as Helen McCabe's Knickerbocker Nursery, and from eminent early twentieth-century botanists, such as C.R. Orcutt and T.S. & K.S. Brandegee. Agaves illustrated in Howard Scott Gentry's classic agave monograph still grow in the garden.

A broad cement path sweeps in grand curves where one views the most developed displays, primarily African succulents and South American cacti. Wandering off onto informal gravel paths that eventually melt into the natural landscape one sees more rustic displays. In this more laid-back part of the garden the most delightful specimens of the Australian bottle tree (*Brachychiton rupestre*) are located. They grow among some rocks, with their squat, gouty trunks up to six feet in diameter. These would be terrific trees for a children's garden because of their resemblance to the baby baobabs that took over the asteroid in Saint-Exupéry's charming story *The Little Prince*.

The plant selection forms a delightful medley of contrasting, sometimes shocking, but mostly complementary, shapes and textures. The garden's primary strength, in addition to enjoying a location near the ocean, is its powerful displays of African succulents in settings of exotic subtropical trees. Some of the trees are palo verde, coral tree, dragon's blood tree, and rare *Dombeya rotundifolia*.

The garden abounds in aloes, perhaps a reflection of its caretaker's passion for succulents. There are enough aloe species and hybrids to guarantee year-round flower displays. I was particularly impressed by a mass planting of the beautiful winter-flowering *Aloe rubroviolacea* from Yemen, where it grows on steep slopes. It was first described at the end of the last century and was growing at La Mortola garden on the Italian Riviera in 1900. It was not grown in the United States until the 1960s, when the undisputed authority on Old World succulents, John Lavranos, recollected it in Yemen. It is truly one of the best garden aloes for California and other Mediterranean gardens. The plants adorn one

mound, and closer inspection indicates that the garden really has a great conservation collection of *A. rubroviolacea*—no two plants are alike, indicating each was grown from seed. The Huntington only has two or three clones and here there are over fifty.

In addition to an abundance of species aloes, Park Boulevard cactus garden is nicely planted with colorful Lampranthus for bright, cheery color, and many large specimens of the shrub and tree euphorbias—*Euphorbia grandicornis*, *E. heptagona* (slowly disappearing from gardens), and *E. ammak*, to name just a few—all composed to give a naturalistic, yet otherwordly, landscape. The African element has a dream-like quality. I wonder if those who carved their initials in the highly toxic *Euphorbia venenata* had nightmares on their way to the emergency room. If the juice got on their hands and they rubbed their eyes they would not see much. While I don't care for graffitti on plants. I do worry about planting euphorbias in public (and private) gardens where visitors might be unaware of the danger of an otherwise inviting plant's toxic properties.

It was a surprise to see in a public park's garden specimens of the South African milk barrel (*E. horrida* var. *noorsveldensis*). Comparable to our Western Hemisphere barrel cactus, the milk barrel is an unusual sight in gardens, though with proper drainage it thrives. Collectors usually grow them in pots and haul them to cactus shows. I like them best when they stay put in the garden.

Along the escarpment behind the cactus garden are numerous plantings of agaves; the silvery-gray-leaved *Agave*

americana and *A. franzosenii* are very imposing on the steep hillsides. The agaves become more plentiful as one walks in the direction of the zoo parking lot. Again, a gardener took a liking to a genus and collected and planted them, undoubtedly with the help of Howard Scott Gentry. Such diversity in a public garden cries out for labels that identify the species—a good project for the San Diego Cactus and Succulent Society, which meets in a nearby auditorium at the park. There are specimens of the seldom seen *Furcraea macdougallii*. The genus *Furcraea* is closely related to Agave, but has much thinner and longer leaves, and the flowers, produced on gigantic terminal treelike inflorescences, are pendent, not upright. *F. macdougallii* is from central Mexico and is one of the tallest of the genus. The plant and its flower stalk combined may reach forty to fifty feet.

The sections of the garden dedicated to the cacti of Mexico and South America are, unfortunately, not as well represented as the African succulents. The very small South America planting contains interesting specimens of tubular-flowered shrubby cacti, including *borzicactus*, *cleistocactus*, and *morawetzia*—but these are outclassed by the robust armies of South African aloes, euphorbias, and mesembs. Since Mexico is just a few miles away, I expected to see stronger displays and better landscaping, particularly for the native cacti and succulents of Baja California. However, at the San Diego's Zoo's Wild Animal Park in Escondido, one can see the finest Baja display outside of Baja. In many respects it is superior to the one I did years ago at the Huntington; its sheer size (about four acres) and vast inventory of succulents make the visitor feel as if in the Vizcaino Desert in central Baja.

Another odd feature near the entrance is the copal plant (*Bursera hindsiana*) used as a clipped hedge along an entry path from the boulevard. It is more decorative and useful in gardens as a shrub or small tree. Here it is clipped and kept about two feet high. Actually, the euphorbias need an inert barrier more than the cacti. Another inconsistency is a Madagascar palm growing among golden barrel cacti from Mexico. This just does not work. There are many cactus specimens native to both North and South America; some *cleistocactus* are nicely grown and their spines are afire in the late afternoon sun, giving them and many of the other spiny cacti an incredible golden glow.

Along the edge of the garden is small grove of dragon's blood trees that makes such a fine composition that it puts one into a landscape painting. The Canary Islands has contributed much to Southern California gardening and landscaping, but the legendary dragon's blood tree, once thought to be the dragon that guards the golden apples of the Gardens of the Hesperides, has no equal. It was introduced, probably at Santa Barbara, as early as the 1850s, and has remained an icon of parks and gardens throughout Southern California.

The Park Boulevard Cactus Garden is part of the San Diego Park and Recreation Department, and on the fourth Saturday of each month a desert garden walk is conducted by a park ranger. At that time one has the opportunity to learn a great deal more about both the park and the garden.

Torch cactus (*Cleistocactus hildegardiae*) from Bolivia.

Index

A
Abrams, LeRoy 70
abromeitiella 57
A California Flora 70
Aeonium arboreum 'Zwartkop' 60, 111, 114
Aesculus 'Canyon Pink' 73
African iris (*Dietes vegeta*) 29
Agave aff. *titanota* 54
Agave americana 171
Agave americana 'Picta' 66
Agave americana var. *medio picta* 'Alba' 98, 118
Agave angustifolia 126
Agave bracteosa 82
Agave ceslii var. *albicans* 81
Agave chrysoglossa 81
Agave ferox 31, 88, 160
Agave franzosinii 39, 46, 118, 171
Agave guiengola 114
Agave horrida 141, 149
Agave 'Leopoldii II' 108
Agave mapisaga var. *lisa* 69, 84, 144
Agave ocahui 56, 57
Agave parryi var. *truncata* 64, 86, 141
Agaves of North America 84
Agave tecta 84
Agave tequilana 86
airplane propeller plant (*Crassula falcata*) 91
Albert S. White Park 12
Alluadia procera 146
Aloe africana 29
Aloe brevifolia 45, 49
Aloe cameronii 111, 158, 162
Aloe camperi 91
Aloe capitata 154
Aloe ciliaris 157
Aloe dorotheae 158
Aloe elgonica 111
Aloe ferox 146, 161
Aloe 'Hercules' 118, 154
Aloe marlothii 88, 154, 160
Aloe microstigma 158
Aloe morogoroensis 158
Aloe mutabilis 31
Aloe nobilis 18
Aloe peglerae 154
Aloe porphyrostachys 158
Aloe pseudorubroviolacea 160
Aloe 'Rooikapie' ('Red Head') 91
Aloe ramosissima 45
Aloe rubroviolacea 146, 158, 160, 165, 169, 170
Aloe 'Sailor's Warning' 30
Aloe scabrifolia 114
Aloe spectabilis 160
Aloe striata 25–26, 151, 154
Aloe suprafoliata 154
Aloe thraskii 31, 158
Aloe ukambensis 158
Aloe vanbalenii 158
Aloe vaombe 118
Aloe vera 50, 94
Aloe 'William Hertrich' 30
Anderson, Patrick 11, 151
The Arid Conquest of America 9
Arizona fish hook barrel (*Ferocactus wislizenii*) 114
Arizona rainbow (*Echinocereus pectinatus* var. *rigidissimus*) 64
saguaro (*Carnegiea gigantea*) 137

astrophytum 57
Attiret, Jean 15
autumn sage (*Salvia greggii*) 54
Aztec column cactus (*Neobuxbaumia polylopha*) 39, 144, 149

B
Bailey, Liberty Hyde 70
Balboa Park Cactus Gardens 166–173
baobab (*Adansonia digitata*) 160
Barbaro, Lynne Deane 144
Barrel cactus (*ferocactus*) 57
beargrass (*Nolina parryi* ssp. *wolfii*) 73
Beaucarnea stricta 50
Benson, Lyman 50
Berger, Alwin 15
Berger, Fritz 15
Biltmore Hotel, Santa Barbara 18
bishop's cap cactus (*Astrophytum myriostigma*) 146
Bixby, John W. 70
Bixby Bryant, Suzanna 70
blue barrel (*Ferocactus glaucescens*) 141, 149
blue euphorbia (*Euphorbia coerulescens*) 146
blue kleinia (*Senecio mandraliscae*) 34, 46, 60, 98, 103
boojum trees (*Fouquieria columnaris*) 84
borzicactus 29, 91, 114, 171
Borzicactus (*Hildewintera*) *aureispinus* 25, 86
Borzicactus tessellatus 114
bottle palm (*Beaucarnea recurvata*) 50
bottle tree (*Brachychiton rupestre*) 162, 169
Bradury estate 76
Brandegee, K.S. 169
Brandegee, T.S. 169
Braunton, Ernest 70, 114
Brazilian lemon ball cactus (*Notocactus leninghausii*) 40, 54
brittlebush (*Encelia farinosa*) 133
Bullard Memorial Cactus Garden 126
Burbank, Luther 34
burro tail (*Sedum morganianum*) 58
Bursera microphylla 66, 126

C
Cacti for the Amateur 13
Cactus and Succulent Society of America 13, 50, 130
California: A Book for Travellers and Settlers 9
California Academy of Sciences 82, 130
California as Health and Resort 9
California buckeye (*Aesculus californica*) 73
California Cactus Growers Association 130
California desert fan palm (*Washingtonia filifera*) 132
California Gardens 39
California juniper (*Juniperus californica*) 72
California lilac (*Ceanothus megacarpus*) 74
California sycamore (*Platanus racemosa*) 149
cane cholla (*Opuntia imbricata*) 66, 74
Cape Aloe (*Aloe arborescens*) 12, 94, 157
Catalan, Raymond 94
Catlin, Jack 111

century plant (*Agave americana*) 12, 39, 54, 94, 103
Cereus hildmannianus 60
chalk plant (*Dudleya brittonii*) 73
chalk plant (*Dudleya pulverulenta*) 144, 146
Chicago Botanic Garden 74
Chilean wine palm (*Jubaea chilensis*) 36
chin cactus (*Gymnocalycium horstii*) 50, 56
torch cactus (*cleistocactus*) 86, 91, 114, 117, 171, 172
Cleistocactus wendeliorum 31
Clements, Joe 84, 94, 108
coast cholla (*Opuntia prolifera*) 74
coast live oak (*Quercus agrifolia*) 149
Cohen, Laura 149
Coleman, Ronald 122
compass barrel (*Ferocactus cylindraceus, F. acanthodes*) 14
Connor, Wayne 137
Convention on Biological Diversity (CBD) 8, 14
Convention on International Trade in Endangered Species (CITES) 8, 14
Cooper, Elwood 30
copal plant (*bursera hindsiana*) 172
coral tree (*Erythrina*) 110, 113
Cornell, Ralph Dalton 70, 126
Corryocactus ayacuchoensis 98
coryphantha 57
cottontop cactus (*Echinocactus polycephalus*) 14
Cotyledon orbiculata 60
cow's horn euphorbia (*Euphorbia grandicornis*) 60, 170
cow's tongue (*Opuntia lindheimeri* var. *linguiformis*) 94, 98
Crassula arborescens 68
Crassula 'Camp Fire' 146
Crassula erosula 60
creosote bush (*Larrea divaricata*) 132
Crosby, Bing 126
Cyphostemma juttae 86

D
date palm (*Phoenix dactylifera*) 132, 137
de Forest, Lockwood 39
de Laet, Franz 76
desert agave (*Agave deserti*) 132
Desert Plant Life 13–14, 29
devil cactus (*Stenocereus eruca*) 149
Disney, Walt 126, 130
Dobyns, Winifrid 39
Doheny estate 76
Dombeya wallichii 168, 169
Dracaena serrulata 86
dragon's blood tree (*Dracaena draco*) 36, 40, 44, 50, 66, 81, 91, 106, 169, 172
dyckia 92, 114
dymmondia 151

E
Easter lily (*echinopsis*) 91
Eastwood, Alice 70
echeveria 46, 57
Echeveria 'Perle von Nurnburg' 103
Echeveria 'Doris Taylor' 149
Echeveria 'Pinky' 154
Echinocereus pectinatus 162
elephant bush (*Portulacaria afra* 'Variegated') 60
elephant's foot (*Dioscorea*) 88

Englemann, George 12
Eriogonum 'Shasta Sulfur' 73
Euphorbia ammak 170
Euphorbia fruticosa 50
Euphorbia grandicornis 94
Euphorbia heptagona 170
Euphorbia lambii 91, 108
Euphorbia milii var. *hislopii* 91, 108, 111
Euphorbia milii 'Apache Red' 91, 111
Euphorbia resinifera, 114, 120
Euphorbia rigida 157
Euphorbia 'Sticks on Fire' 103
Euphorbia tetragona 94
Euphorbia tirucalli 94
Euphorbia venenata 170
Euphorbia xantii 66, 146
Evans, Mike 140

F
False Agave (*hechtia*) 114
Fan Aloe (*Aloe plicatilis*) 49, 106, 113
Farrand, Beatrix 70
Favel, Phil 160, 162
felt tree (*Kalanchoe beharensis*) 108
Ferocactus rectispinus 84
Festuca cineria (*F. glauca*) 108
Fick, Amy 58
Fick Garden 58–63
Fick, Otto 58
Fick, Virginia 58
floss silk tree (*Chorisia speciosa*) 58
Folsom, James 84, 92
Foster, Robert 45
foxtail agave (*Agave attenuata*) 20, 25
Franceschi, Francesco 18
Frank Jordano Garden 28–35
Fremont, John C. 12
Furcraea macdougallii 151, 171
Furcraea selloa marginata 108

G
Ganna Walska Lotusland 36–49
garambullo (*myrtillocactus*) 146
Garbo, Greta 122
Garden of Acclimatization 18
Gary Lyons Garden 50–57
Gates, Howard 50, 130
Gavitt, E.P. 36
Gentry, Howard Scott 46, 84, 86, 171
Gerardanthus macrorhizus 114
Getty Center 8, 9, 11
Getty Center Cactus Garden 100–105
Glass, Charles 45
golden barrel (*Echinocactus grusonii*) 10, 36, 82, 84, 103
Golden Gate Park, San Francisco 82
Goodspeed, T. Harper 84
Graptopetalum fittkaui 84
Graptopetalum paraguayense 60
great basin sagebrush (*Artemisia tridentata*) 74
Griffith Park 14
Grigsby, Dave 146
Gunther Schwartz Garden 18–27, 30

H
Haage, Adolph 13
Haage and Schmidt nursery 76
Hanbury, Thomas Sir 14
Harris, Phil 126
Haselton, Scott 13, 50
Haworthia gracilis 111
hedgehog (*echinocereus*) 10, 14, 57, 160, 165
Hercules club (*Euphorbia canariensis*)

146, 170

Hertrich, William 11, 13–15, 39, 76, 84
Heveron, Dave 136
Hildewintera aureispina 60
Hosp, F.P. 13
Hummel, E.C. 91
Huntington Desert Garden 8–11, 13, 15, 20, 29–31, 64, 76–93, 101, 108, 126, 130, 151, 158, 160, 170, 171
Huntington, Glenn 137
Huntington, Henry E. 10, 70, 76
Huntington Ranch 14

I

An illustrated Guide to the Flowers of Saudi Arabia 158
impala lily (*Adenium obesum*) 137
Indian fig cactus (*Opuntia ficus indica*) 12, 94
International Succulent Introductions (ISI) 82
ironwood tree (*Olneya tesota*) 137
Irwin, Robert 103

J

James, George Wharton 122
Jepson, Willis Linn 70
Jordano, Frank 29
Johnson, Harry 50, 54
Johnson's Water and Cactus Gardens 13
Joshua Tree National Park 126
Joshua tree (*Yucca brevifolia*) 10, 14, 74
Journal of the Cactus and Succulent Society of America 13, 45, 50, 82
Jung, Carl 36, 114

K

kalanchoe 46
Kalanchoe fedtschenkoi 106
kangaroo paw (*Anigozanthos*) 103
kapok tree (*ceiba*) 58
karoo acacia (*Acacia karoo*) 146
Kimnach, Myron 84

L

La Mortola 14–15, 169
lampranthus 20, 23
Lampranthus 'Gold Nugget' 151
Lavranos, John 169
lemon ball cactus (*Notocactus leninghausii*) 60
Letts, Arthur 14
Lindsay, George 130
Linné, Carl (Carolus Linnaeus) 11
Living Desert Wildlife and Animal Park 10, 126, 130, 132–139
living rock cactus (*Ariocarpus kotschubeyanus*) 12
Lobivia 'Glorious' 146
Lord's candle (*Y. whipplei*) 146
Los Angeles Zoo 8, 64–69
Lyon and Cobbe 13

M

Madagascar palm (*Pachypodium lameri*) 20, 26, 94
madrone (*Arbutus menziesi*) 73
Mahonia 'Golden Abundance' 73
Mammillaria backebergii 88
McCabe, Helen 169
medicinal aloe (*Aloe vera*) 12, 146
The Mediterranean Shores of America 9
Meier, Richard 101
Mexican bird of paradise (*Caesalpinia mexicana*) 54, 137
Mildred Mathias Botanical Garden 31
milk barrel 54, 114

milk barrel (*Euphorbia horrida*) 114, 117, 146
milk barrel (*Euphorbia horrida* var. *noorsveldensis*) 170
mission cactus (*Opuntia ficus indica*) 151
Missouri Botanical Garden 13
Modelo Shales 106–113
Mojave Desert cholla 10
monkey thorn (*Acacia galpinii*) 137
Monterey cypress 36
Moorten Botanical Garden 10, 122–131
Moorten, Chester "Cactus Slim" 122, 126
Moorten, Clark 122, 126
Moorten, Jason 122
Moorten, Pat 122, 130
Munz, Phillip 70
mytillocactus 130
Nelson, Helen 94, 98
Neobuxbaumia scoparia 86
Newcomber, Don 114, 121
New York Botanical Garden 13
New Zealand flax (*Phormium tenax*) 30
Nickels, Anna B. 11
night-blooming cereus (*Cereus xanthocarpus*) 81
Nolan, Stephen 12
Nolina parryi ssp. *wolfii* 72
Nordhoff, Charles 9
Notocactus magnificus 54, 149
Nyctocereus serpentinus 60

O

O'Brien, Bart 73
ocotillo 14
ombu tree (*Phytolacca dioica x P. weberbaueri*) 20
Olin, Laurie 101
Olmsted, Frederick Law, Jr. 70
O'Neill, Donna 140, 144
O'Neill Garden 10–11, 16–17, 140–149
O'Neill, Richard 140
Opuntia erinacea var. *ursina* 'Mike Hammit' 73
Opuntia megacantha 94
Opuntia spinulifera 18
Opuntia vaseyi 73
Orcutt, C.R. 169

P

pachycaul 57
pachyphytum 57
palmilla (*Yucca elata*) 137
palo adán (*Fouquieria macdougallii*) 50
Palos Verdes Estates 70
palo verde tree (*Parkinsonia aculeata*) 137
Parkinsidium 'Desert Museum' 73
pasacana (*Trichocereus pasacana*) 151
Paseck, John 169
Patrick Anderson Garden 151–157
Payne, Theodore 70
perfume acacia (*Acacia caven*) 146
Persian slipper (*Pedilanthus macrocarpus*) 66
Peruvian pepper tree (*Schinus molle*) 151
Peruvian old woman cactus (*Espostoa melanostele*) 149
Phil Favel Garden 8, 29, 158–165
Pico, Pio 140
pilosocereus 30
Pilosocereus azureus 34
pincushion cactus (*mammillaria*) 54, 57, 84
pipe organ cactus (*Pachycereus*

marginatus) 144
pitahaya (*Stenocereus weberi*) 130
pitcairnea 92
pony tail palm (*Beaucarnea recurvata*) 44
Popenoe, Wilson 135
Portola Expedition 149
Plant Hunters in the Andes 84
prickly pear (*Opuntia macrocentra*) 137
prickly pear (*Opuntia streptacantha*) 64, 103
Pride of Madeira (*Echium fastuosum*) 29, 157
Proscewicz, Teresa 69
pulque 69
puya 92
Puya alpestris 98
Puya berteroniana 86
pyracantha 58

Q

Queen Victoria agave (*Agave victoriae reginae*) 46, 146
quiver tree (*Aloe dichotoma*) 45, 88, 154, 158

R

rainbow cactus (*Echinocereus dasyacanthus*) 64
Rancho Los Alamitos 70
Rancho Mission Viejo 140
Reinelt, Frank 34
Remondino, P.C. 9
Rhadwa Aloe 158
Riedel, Peter 36
Riverside Mission Inn 13
R.J. O'Neill Ranch 70
Rooksby, Ellen 13–14

S

Saint-Exupéry, Antoine Marie Roger de 54, 169
Salvia 'Pozo Blue' 73
Sanders, F.C.S. 9
San Diego Cactus and Succulent Society 171
San Diego Zoo and Wild Animal Park 171
San Gabriel Mission 15, 94–99, 151
San Juan Capistrano Mission 146
San Pedro cactus (*Trichocereus pachanoi*) 103
Santa Barbara Acclimatization Association 30
Santa Barbara Botanic Garden 30
Santa Barbara Mission 30
Sargent Charles Sprague 70
Schick hybrids 91
Schick, Robert 91
sedum 46
Sedum rubrotinctum 146
Semi-Tropical California 9
Sennett, Mack 126
Senecio vitalis 98
Serra Gardens 114–121
Serra, Junipero 94
Sessions, Kate O. 166, 169
Sexton, Joseph 30
Sher, Abby 111
Skelton, Red 126
siempreviva (*Dudleya brittonii*) 66, 103
Sinatra, Frank 126
silver dollar prickly pear (*Opuntia robusta*) 144, 145

smoke tree (*Dalea*) 132
Smythe, William 9–10
Socotran fig (*Ficus socotrana*) 160
Southern California 9
Spanish dagger yucca (*Yucca gloriosa*) 14
squirting cucumber (*Ecballium elaterium*) 20
statice (*Limonium perezii*) 54
Stenocereus thurberi var. *littoralis* 130
Stevens, R. Kinton 36, 40
Stevens, Ralph 39
Swanson, Gloria 122
Succulents for the Amateur 13

T

Taylor, Roy 74
teddy bear cholla (*O. bigelovii*) 14
Tegelberg, Gil, Jr. 126, 130
thelocactus 57, 160
Thomas, Warren 64
torch cactus (*Cleistocactus strausii*) 37, 60
torch cactus (*Cleistocactus hildegardiae*) 173
totem pole cactus (*Lophocereus schotti* 'Monstrose') 73
Trichocereus pasacana 34
Trager, John 82
Traveler's Palm (*Ravenala madagascariensis*) 20
tree aloe (*Aloe bainesii*) 31, 88, 113, 114, 118, 154
tree euphorbia (*Euphorbia ingens*) 34, 40, 49, 103, 114, 166
tree nolina (*Nolina beldingii*) 106
tree yucca (*Yucca filifera*) 81, 85, 106
trichocereus 36
trichocereus (*echinopsis*) 20, 34
Trichocereus terscheckii 34
Truman, Benjamin 9

U

U.S. Bureau of Plant Introduction 137
U.S. Department of Agriculture 14
U.S. Endangered Species Act 8, 14

V

Van Der Stel, Simon 158
verbena 151
Verity, David 31
Van Dyke, Theodore S. 9

W

Walker, Boyd 106
Walker, Mary Ev 106
Walker, William C. 12
Walska, Ganna 36, 39, 40, 45, 47
Walther, Eric 82
Warren and Sons 12
Weinberg, F. 13
Weld, Rogers 144
Wemple, Emmet 101
White Park Garden 10, 13
white thorn (*A. albida*) 137
Wigginsia sellowii (*Parodia erinacea*) 91
The Wonders of the Colorado Desert 122

Y

Yucca gloriosa 22
Yucca thompsoniana 146
Yucca whipplei 71

Public Garden Directory

Ganna Walska Lotusland
695 Ashley Road
Santa Barbara, CA 93108
Reservations for docent-guided 1 1/2–2-hour walking tour Wednesday through Saturday mid February through mid November
For reservations call (805) 969-9990

Los Angeles City Zoo [Located in Griffith Park at the junction of the Ventura (134) and the Golden Gate (I-5) freeways.]
5333 Zoo Drive
Los Angeles, CA 90027 (323) 644-6400
Hours: 10:00 am to 5:00 pm daily except December 25. Saturdays and Sundays in July and Auguest, open until 6:00 pm. Admission $8.25 adults, $3.25 for children ages 2–12.

Rancho Santa Ana Botanic Garden
1500 N. College Ave.
Claremont, CA 91711 (909) 625-8767
Hours: daily 8:00 am to 5 pm. Admission is free.

Huntington Library, Art Gallery, and Botanical Gardens
1151 Oxford Road
San Marino, CA 91108 (626) 405-2141
Hours: 1–4:30 pm Tuesday–Friday; 10:30 am to 4:30 pm Saturday and Sunday; closed Mondays and major holidays. Admission: adults $8:50; seniors $8.00; students $6.00; children under 12 free. Admission is free the first Thursday of each month.

San Gabriel Mission
428 South Mission Drive
San Gabriel, CA 91776 (626) 457-3048
Hours: 9 am to 4:30 pm daily; closed most holidays. Admission for adults over 12 $4.00; children 6–12 $1.00. Guided tours available for parties of 25 or more.

The Getty Center
1200 Getty Center Drive
Los Angeles, CA 90049
(310) 440-7300, for advance parking reservations ($5.00) and information; visitors planning to arrive by bus or shuttle may not need reservations, but check before departure. Visiting hours are Tuesday and Wednesday 11 am to 7 pm, Thursday and Friday 11 am to 9 pm, and Saturday and Sunday 10 am to 6 pm. Closed Mondays and major holidays. Admission is free.

The Living Desert
47-900 Portola Ave.
Palm Desert, CA 92260
(760) 346-5694
Hours are 9 am to 5 pm from September 1 through June 15 and 8 am to noon June 16 through July 31. Admission: adults $7.50; seniors $6.50; children 3–12 $3.50; 2 and younger free.

Moorten Botanical Garden
1701 South Canyon Drive
Palm Springs, CA 92264 (760) 317-6555
Hours: 9–4:30 Monday through Saturday; Sundays 10–4 pm; closed most holidays; facilities available for weddings and receptions, classes, tours, exhibits, and other events offered.

Balboa Park Desert Garden
Garden located on the far east side of Balboa Park, along Park Blvd., across the street from the parking lots for the San Diego Zoo and the San Diego Natural History Museum.
Hours: open every day 365 days a year.
For visitor information about the cactus garden, including tours, other gardens, museums, and zoo, call (619) 229-0512; (619) 235-1100; (619) 236-5717.

Bibliography

Adams, Emma H. To and fro in Southern California. W.M.B.C. Press: Cincinnati, 1887.

Adams, William Howard. Grounds for Change: Major Gardens in the Twentieth Century. Boston: Little, Brown & Co., 1993.

"Albert White Park, Riverside," Desert Plant Life 2 (1931): 151–152.

Anderson, Miles. The Ultimate Book of Cacti and Succulents. New York: Lorenz Books, 1998.

Attiret, Jean Deni. A Particular Account of the Emperor of China's Gardens. Translated by Sir Harry Beaumont. London, 1752.

Balthis, Frank K. "A Succulent House at Garfield Park Conservatory," Desert Plant Life 2 (1930): 15–16.

Baumgartner, Jerome W. Rancho Santa Margarita Remembered. Santa Barbara: Fithian Press, 1989.

Benson, Lyman, and Robert Darrow. Trees and Shrubs of the Southwestern Deserts, 3rd edition. Tucson: University of Arizona Press, 1981.

Britton, Nathaniel Lord, and Joseph Nelson Rose. The Cactaceas, 4 vols. Pasadena: Abbey Garden Press, 1937.

Brookbank, George E. Desert Landscaping. Tucson: University of Arizona Press, 1992.

Brown-Folsom, D. Dry Climate Gardening with Succulents. New York: Panteon Books, 1995.

Clarke, Charlotte Bringle. Edible and Useful Plants of California. Berkeley and Los Angeles: University of California Press, 1977.

Corlett, Dudley S. "Conservation and the Botanic Garden," Desert Plant Life 2 (1930): 45–46.

Crawford, Sharon. Ganna Walska Lotusland. Santa Barbara: Companion Press, 1996.

Dallman, Peter R. Plant Life in the World's Mediterranean Climates. Berkeley and Los Angeles: University of California Press, 1998.

Dearholt, S. Ray. "A Desert Landscape in the Home Garden," Desert Plant Life 1 (1929): 93.

Dobyns, Winifred Starr. California Gardens. New York: The MacMillan Company, 1931.

Downing, Andrew Jackson. Rural Essays. New York: Leavitt & Allen, 1855.

Duffield, Mary Rose, and Warren D. Jones. Plants for Dry Climates. Los Angeles: HP Books, 1992.

Ebeling, Walter. Handbook of Indian Foods and Fibers of Arid America. Berkeley and Los Angeles: University of California Press, 1986.

Eberts, Mike. Griffith Park: A Centennial History. Los Angeles: Historical Society of Southern California, 1996.

Elder, Paul. The Old Spanish Missions of California. San Francisco: Paul Elder & Co., 1913.

Everett, Percy C. A Summary of the Culture of California Plants at the Rancho Santa Ana Botanic Gardens, 1927–1950. Claremont: Rancho Santa Ana Botanic Garden Publishing Group, 1957.

Francis, Mark, and Andreas Relmann. The California Landscape Garden: Ecology, Culture, and Design. Berkeley and Los Angeles: University of California Press, 1999

French, Jere Stuart. The California Garden. Washington, D.C.: The Landscape Architecture Foundation, 1993.

Gardener, T.R. II. Lotusland: A Photographic Odyssey. Santa Barbara: Allen A. Knoll, 1995.

"Gardening in the Big League," San Diego Union Tribune (January 31, 1998).

Gentry, Howard Scott. The Agaves of Continental North America. Tucson, University of Arizona Press, 1982.

Gilmer, Maureen. The Complete Guide to Southern California Gardening. Dallas: Taylor Publishing Company, 1995.

Hanson, J.W. The American Italy: Southern California. Chicago: W.B. ConkeyCo., 1995.

Hertrich, William. The Huntington Botanical Gardens: Personal Recollections. San Marino: The Huntington Library, 1949.

Houk, Walter. The Botanical Gardens at the Huntington. San Marino: The Huntington Library; New York: Harry N. Abrams, 1996.

"H.P. Hosp, Who Brought to this City Both Fame and Beauty," Desert Plant Life 2 (1951): 151.

Hyams, Williams, and William Macquity. Great Botanical Gardens of the Western World. London: Bloomsbury Books, 1969.

Innes, Clive, and Charles Glass. Cacti. New York: Portland House, 1991.

James, George Wharton. The Wonders of the Colorado Desert. Boston: Little, Brown & Co., 1906.

Jeracek, C.I. "A Plant Paradise: Succulent Gardens of Kate O. Seeions, Horticulturist," Desert Plant Life 3 (1931): 90–91.

Johnson, Eric A. Pruning, Planting and Care. Tucson: Ironwood Press, 1997.

Keator, Glenn. Complete Guide to the Native Perennials of California. San Francisco: Chronicle Books, 1990.

--------. Complete Guide to Native Shrubs of California. San Francisco: Chronicle Books, 1994.

Knopf, Jim. The Xeriscape Flower Gardener. Boulder: Johnson Books, 1991.

Lamb, Samuel H. Woody Plants of the Southwest. Santa Fe: The Sunstone Press, 1975.

Lenz, Lee W. Rancho Santa Ana Botanic Garden: The First Fifty Years, 1927–1977. Claremont: Rancho Santa Ana Botanic Garden, 1977.

Lindley, Walter, and J.P. Widney. California of the South. New York: D. Appelton & Company, 1888.

Lyons, Gary. The Huntington Desert Garden. Pasadena: Abbey Garden Press, 1969.

-------. "In Search of Dragons, or, The Plant that Roared," Cactus and Succulent Journal 46, (1974): 267–282.

-------. "Conservation: A Waste of Time?" Cactus and Succulent Journal 44 (1972): 173–177.

--------. "Divine Nectar," Huntington Library Calendar (January–Feabuary 1976).

-------. "Some New Developments in Conservation," Cactus and Succulent Journal 48 (1978) 155–162.

--------. "The C.S.S.A [Cactus and Succulent Society of America] and Conservation: A Boom or a Bust?" Cactus and Succulent Journal 51 (1979): 9–15.

-------. "The Botanical Garden and the Conservation of Endangered Species," Huntington Library Calendar (November–December 1980).

-------. "At Long Last, Protection for Endangered Cacti," Cactus and Succulent Journal (1980): 52, 229, 232.

---------. "Landscaping with Extinction," Conservation and Commerce of Cacti and Other Succulents. Washington, D.C.: World Wildlife Fund, 226–244.

Mabberly, D.J. The Plant Book, 2nd edition. Cambridge: The Cambridge University Press, 1997.

Mielke, Judy. Native Plants for Southwestern Climates. Austin: University of Texas Press, 1993.

Miller, George O. Landscaping with Native Plants of Texas and the Southwest. Stillwater: Voyager Press, 1991.

Munz, Philipp A. A California Flora and Supplement. Berkeley and Los Angeles: University of California Press, 1973.

----------. A Flora of Southern California. Berkeley and Los Angeles: University of California, 1974.

Nickels, Anna B. Catalogue and Price List: Arcadia Garden. n.d. [ca. 1890].

Nordhoff, Charles. California: For Health, Pleasure, and Residence. New York: Harper & Brothers, 1872.

Padilla, Victoria. Southern California Gardens: An Illustrated History. Berkeley and Los Angeles: University of California Press, 1961.

Palmer, Eve, and Noah Pitman. Trees of Southern Africa. Cape Town: A.A. Balkema, 1972.

Perry, Bob. Landscape Plants for Western Regions. Claremont: Land Design Publishing, 1992.

Philips, Judith. Southwestern Landscaping with Native Plants. Santa Fe: Museum of Mexico Press, 1987.

Power, Nancy Groslee. The Gardens of California. New York: Clarkson Potter Publishers, 1995.

Remondino, P.C. The Mediterranean Shores of America: Southern California. Philadelphia and London: P.A. Davs Co., 1892.

Reynolds, Gilbert W. The Aloes of South Africa. Johannesburg: Aloes of South Africa Book Fund, 1950.

----------. The Aloes of Tropical Africa and Madagascar. Mbalane: The Trustees of the Aloe Book Fund, 1966.

Rowley, Gordon W. A History of Succulent Plants. Mill Valley: Strawberry Press, 1997.

----------. The Illustrated Encyclopedia of Succulents. New York: Crown Publishers, 1978.

Sanders, F.C.S. California as a Health Resort. San Francisco: Bolte & Braden Co., 1916.

Saunders, Charles Francis. Trees and Shrubs of California Gardens. New York: Robert M. McBride & Co., 1926.

Scharf, Thomas, "Balboa Park: A San Diego Botanical Landmark," Pacific Horticulture (September 1988): 54–63.

Shuler, Carol. Low Water Use Plants for California and the Southwest. Tucson: Fisher Books, 1993.

Smaus, Robert. California Gardening. New York: Harry N. Abrams, Inc., 1983.

Smyth, William. The Conquest of Arid America. New York: The MacMillan Company, 1905.

Spain, John N. Growing Winter Hardy Cacti in Cold/Wet Climate Conditions. Waterton, Connecticut: Elizabeth Harmon, 1997.

Streatfield, David C. California Gardens: Creating a New Eden. New York: Abbeville Press, 1994.

Thorpe, James. "The Creation of the Gardens," The Huntington Library Quarterly 32, no. 4 (1969): 333–350.

-----------. Henry Edwards Huntington: A Biography. Berkeley and Los Angeles: University of California Press, 1994.

Truman, Benjamin C. Semi-Tropical California. San Francisco: A.L. Bancroft & Co., 1874.

Van Dyke, John C. The Desert, 2nd Edition. Charles Scribners Sons, 1902.

Van Dyke, Theodore S. Southern California. New York: Fords, Howard & Hulbert, 1885.

van Wyck, Ben-Erik, and Gideon Smith. Guide to the Aloes of South Africa. Pretoria: Briza Publications, 1996.

----------, et al. Medicinal Plants of South Africa. Pretoria: Briza Publications, 1997.

Walters, James E. Shade and Color with Water-Conserving Plants. Portland: Timber Press, 1992.

Warner, Charles Dudley. Our Italy. New York: Harper & Brothers, 1901.

Wasowski, Sally, and Andy Wasowski. Native Gardens for Dry Climates. New York: Clarkson Potter Publishers, 1995.

Watt, John Mitchell, and Maria Gerdina Breyer-Brandwijk. Poisonous and Medicinal Plants of Southern and Eastern Africa, 2nd edition. Edinburgh and London: E. & S. Livingstone, Ltd., 1962